Data for the Tiger
A fable about data culture

By Thomas Gengler

Data for the Tiger

A fable about data culture

By Thomas Gengler

© 2023 Thomas Gengler

1st edition

Cover design & illustration:
Tanja Müller (http://tanjarrrh.com)

Contributing authors: Dr. Carsten Bange
(Chapter „The BARC Data Culture Framework")

Proofreading (of original text in German): Petra Embacher

Translation into English supported by: Deepl

Proofreading of English translation: Tim Ellis & Milica Radojicic

Production and publishing: BoD – Books on Demand, Norderstedt

ISBN Paperback: 9 783741 293214

The work, including its parts, is protected by copyright. Any exploitation is prohibited without the consent of the publisher and the author. This applies in particular to electronic or other reproduction, translation, distribution and making available to the public.

Bibliografische Information der Deutschen Nationalbibliothek:
    Die Deutsche Nationalbibliothek verzeichnet diese Publikation in der Deutschen Nationalbibliografie; detaillierte bibliografische Daten sind im Internet über http://dnb.d-nb.de abrufbar.

Inhaltsverzeichnis

Foreword	6
The Dark Threat	10
The Wake-up Call	14
The Jungle Conference	17
The Strategy of Survival	23
The Magic of the Forest	27
The Visual Revolution	31
The Dolphin's Academy	38
The Elephant's Law	43
The Parrot's Gospel	49
The Harmony of the Rhino	53
The Law of the Strongest	59
The Self-service Animals	63
The Power of Community	68
The Challenge of Diversity	72
The Magic of Lighthouses	78
The Pains of the Tiger	84
A New World	87
The Oracle	92
The Dark Side of Power	98
Lean and Fast	104
The Power of Manipulation	109
The Rescue of the Jungle	114
A New Morning	119
20 Steps to Success	123
The BARC Data Culture Framework	125
Acknowledgements	132

Foreword

Data and analytics is a topic that many companies deal with. Not for nothing is data referred to as the oil or gold of the 21st century. The right information at the right time can make all the difference. And data-based decisions or business models offer completely new opportunities.

Accordingly, there is a vast amount of technical literature on the subject of data, reporting, business intelligence, advanced analytics, etc. These reference books are well-founded, informative and instructive, but often also dry and theoretical.

This is where "Data for the Tiger" is meant to stand out from other technical books. The development of a data culture is not explained here using complex technical terms, but embedded in a story, to be precise, in a fable.

The best thing about it is that it is not a technical or scientific treatise. This book is data culture wrapped up in an animal story that will make you wonder, sympathise, empathise and smile.

This means that this fable reference book is not only suitable for data and analytics experts, for whom it nevertheless provides many suggestions and impulses on how they can improve their data and analytics offerings.

"Data for the Tiger" can equally be used to convince colleagues and data and analytics users from the business units of the benefits of a data-driven company.

The central thesis of this book is that the path to becoming a data-driven company is a long journey, which I would like to take you on with the help of a vivid story in a clear and exemplary way.

As on every journey, there are different ways to reach the destination. The animals discover the world of data step by step and develop a little further with each chapter. I have chosen the order of these developmental steps in a way that I consider purposeful from my experience. But of course it is also possible to follow the path in a different order. In the end, it is always about where you currently stand in your company, what your most important objectives are and which steps offer you the greatest added value at the moment.

Now join the animals of the jungle on their journey through the world of information and experience how a parrot, an elephant, a dolphin and their many companions develop a living data culture in their threatened jungle.

About the Author

Thomas Gengler was born in 1981 in Germany and works as a graduate in business informatics. He lives with his wife and two sons in Strullendorf near Bamberg.

He discovered his passion for writing stories at the age of 18 by writing song lyrics for a Heavy Metal band.

While Gengler was able to celebrate regional successes with humorous novels under the pseudonym Jonas Philipps, he works on short stories and exciting novels under his second pseudonym Tom Davids.

He acted as editor for a fundraising book against cancer.

His main job has been with a pan-European health service provider since September 2002, where he completed his dual studies as a business informatics graduate (BA). From 2009 to 2021, he led the BI team of Corporate IT and has been responsible for the reporting solutions in the new international data and analytics domain as "Head of Reporting & BI Solutions" since 2022.

"Data for the Tiger" is Gengler's first project combining his passion for writing novels and stories with his professional role as a data and analytics expert.

Further information:
www.linkedin.com/in/thomas-gengler-50738b226/
www.jonas-philipps.de/
www.tom-davids.de/

Introduction BARC

Since its foundation in 1999, BARC has been helping managers to make the right decisions on the successful use of data and analytics. The range of services includes studies, events and consulting: BARC user surveys, software tests and analyst assessments in blogs and research notes give you the confidence to make the right decisions. With its independent research, BARC gets to the heart of market developments and puts software and providers through their paces, so that you can be given valuable impulses on how to turn data, analytics and AI into added value and successfully transform your business.

Leading minds and companies come together at their events. BARC conferences, seminars, experience-sharing circles and online webinars bring information, inspiration and interactivity to more than 10,000 participants every year. Through the exchange with peers and the overview of trends and market developments, you receive new impulses for your business.

The BARC Advisory Practice is all about turning your company's requirements and needs into future-proof decisions. BARC provides you with holistic concepts on the basis of which you can successfully implement your data and analytics strategy and culture as well as architecture and technology. BARC's goal is not to become a long-term implementer with you. Rather, BARC complements your teams with research and experience-based expert input and accompanies you in the successful use of data and analytics, from strategy to optimised data-driven business processes. This includes data strategy and data culture, software selection, architecture, organisation, review and optimisation of the status quo as well as design thinking and use cases.

Part 1

… in which the animals of the forest set the first course for a data-driven jungle in the face of threats to their habitat.

The Dark Threat

The silverback pricked up his ears in concern. He had never heard sounds like these before. They were different from the calls of the animals, unnatural and oppressive. He could not grasp the threat, but he felt it in his enormous chest.

With gentle eyes, he let his gaze wander over the nervous family group. The female gorillas cradled their offspring in their arms and looked around the jungle uneasily. The juvenile males, who otherwise drummed confidently on their chests, avoided his eyes and yawned uncertainly.

Sadly, the gorilla closed his eyes. It could not go on like this. He went to his son, a big, strong gorilla of 13 years. The first grey hairs ran through his black fur. Soon he would be old enough to start a family of his own. But today it was time to teach him to take responsibility.

"Come with me, my son. We have to get to the bottom of this."

"Yes, father."

And so the two gorillas set off, leaving their terrified family behind.

The two gorillas struggled on all fours through the densely overgrown jungle. The muffled sounds grew louder and louder.

"Father, there is a river ahead."

The silverback stopped and straightened up. Searchingly, he looked around. The trees were tall, but too far apart.

"We have to cross it on foot."

He broke off a thick branch and carefully checked the depth of the water. The river was not deep, but it was raging fast.

"Are you strong enough, my son?"

"Of course, father. I can do it!"

Cautiously, the gorillas groped their way to the riverbank and stepped into the cool water on two legs. With a strained grunt, they braced their muscular hind legs against the strong current.

The boy swayed and his father prepared to support him with his strong paws. *But you will do it alone,* he thought proudly. Shortly afterwards, the silverback and his son climbed to the saving shore on the other side and continued their way through the dense undergrowth of the jungle.

The sounds became louder and louder. It was rhythmic. Unreal. As if from another world.

"What can it be, father?"

"I don't know, my son. I've never heard anything like it here in our jungle."

"Do you think it's evil?"

The silverback smiled good-naturedly. "No creature is evil by nature. We all just strive to preserve our habitat and our species and to find enough food. And everyone has found their own way to achieve this goal. Fangs and claws, cunning or strength, speed or deception. Many creatures have different talents than us gorillas. But that doesn't make them evil."

"I understand that, father. But that doesn't sound like an animal looking for food."

Worried, the silverback closed his eyes. "I know, my son," he murmured softly. "That's why we have to reveal the secret."

Cautiously, the two gorillas stalked the deafening noise. They sniffed, listened, and took in their surroundings with all their fine senses. There was an acrid, heavy haze in the air. A smell they could not identify. It seemed artificial and did not fit at all into this jungle.

Slowly they felt their way through the undergrowth, heading unerringly for a towering group of trees.

"Up there," the silverback decided. "We have a better view from there."

The gorillas grasped the tree trunks with their four hands and feet and spread their big toes. They climbed nimbly into the treetop and settled on massive branches that could easily support their impressive weight.

Angrily, the silverback bared his teeth. "Humans!" he growled. A tear ran down his hairy face and dripped from the tree to the ground. His son yawned in bewilderment and stared at the trail of devastation with wide eyes.

He could not count the number of human beings. No family group had such an enormous size. They swarmed in groups, carrying loud, smelly objects in their hands.

"They must be wizards."

"Yes," whispered the silverback. "Not even an enraged elephant can cut down a tree trunk in such a short time."

It was a depressing sight. The trees were bending like blades of grass in the wind. And within a few minutes, humans had cut a deep swath.

"They are destroying our jungle!"

"But what for?" cried the son.

"None of us understands humans."

With a loud rumble, colossal creatures thundered towards them. Their shiny coloured skin reflected the sun, and in the midst of the creatures sat humans.

The young gorilla trembled. "What is that?"

"I don't know, my son," the father replied, having to watch the gigantic creatures punching holes in the earth with brute force. "I don't know ..."

Suddenly, loud shouts rang out. The silverback's eyes flashed in horror. The humans waved their hands and pointed excitedly in the direction of their treetops.

"They've spotted us."

"What should we do, father?"

Then the humans pointed long staffs at them.
And a deafening bang sounded.

Practical application:
Already in the first chapter, the animals of the jungle are threatened existentially.

The modern business world is also teeming with external influences that can pose an existential threat to a company.

Competitors threaten the business habitat, new competitors push into rapidly changing markets, disruptive innovations replace established industries with new technologies and business models.

There are many examples of these rapid developments.

When was the last time you went to a video store? And when was the last time you streamed a movie?

Did you buy your last electronics item from a specialist retailer, or on an eCommerce platform on the Internet?

When did you last insert a CD into a CD player?

Disruptive innovations have always existed. The car replaced the horse step by step. Steam technology once revolutionised the means of transport. But disruptive innovation has never been more fast-moving than in the age of digitalisation.

For companies that do not adapt to these new circumstances, digitalisation can quickly pose a threat. Companies whose business model is based on traditional ways and not on digital technologies are particularly vulnerable.

The two gorillas in our story are completely at a loss in the face of the new situation. Act differently from the brave gorillas. Be prepared!

What opportunities arise in your industry from digitalisation? Where can you become more efficient through the use of digital technologies or optimise your customer offerings? Which new markets or customer groups can be opened up digitally?

The Wake-up Call

The parrot looked up. A distant whirring sound reached his ear. It did not sound like a swarm of bees, but more piercing and dangerous. Puzzled, he waggled his head. If he listened carefully, he could make out other sounds. A dull rumbling.

Worried, he let his eyes wander over the trees. Concentrated on the fine vibrations of the branch on which he was sitting. Nothing but the gentle sway of the wind. He looked up at the sky. No flocks of birds. No panicked attempts to flee. No sign of a tremor in the earth.

"But what on earth makes such noises?" he muttered to himself. He tapped his right shoulder with his left wing. "If this parrot doesn't figure it out, the animals in the jungle will die in stupidity. That's how it is!"

The parrot swung over the high treetops of the jungle, whizzed through the air and followed the source of the noise. He delighted in the colourful bromeliads that grew high in the treetops of the rainforest. Sucked the scent of the mahogany trees into his nose. "How beautiful it is here. Worthy of a magnificent parrot like me," he rejoiced happily.

The sounds became louder. He approached quickly. "Now let's see who's up to no good ..." The words stuck in his throat. The gruesome sight left the parrot speechless, which was extremely rare. With trembling feet, he landed in the nearest treetop and stared at the deep aisle that stretched as far as the eye could see in front of him. Never in his life had he seen such devastation. Dying trees. Destroyed nature. Churned earth. Boundless destruction ...

"Who ... who is capable of such a thing?" *No animal in the jungle would do such a thing.*

Then his sharp eyes spotted a crowd of humans in the distance, digging the ground armed with tools. "Humans," he growled from the depths of his soul that it almost sounded like the growl of a tiger. "I should have guessed ..."

His eyes sparkled. He had to do something. The jungle had to know about this danger. *And who better than me to warn the world!*

Energetically he opened his wings and soared into the air, circled for a brief moment above the swathe of doom, and flew away.

His first target was the gorilla's family, who lived closest to the site of the unimaginable events. Had they not yet noticed the impending disaster? Were they ignorantly living so close to the abyss? The parrot had to talk to the silverback. He was caring and wise. Together with him, he could discuss how to proceed.

When he reached the camp of the gorillas, he first sat down on a branch and got an overview of the situation. The sight tore his heart apart. The young were clinging tiredly to their mothers' fur. The large, otherwise strong apes looked hungry and emaciated. A sad shadow of their former selves. There was no trace of the mighty silverback.

Upset, he settled down in the middle of the rocky clearing. The blank stares of the gorillas were directed at him.

"I need to speak to the silverback urgently."

His wife, the oldest female gorilla of the family band, slowly approached him. Her voice was warm but strangely feeble. "He is not here. We lost him."

"Lost?"

"Yes, lost." A lone tear trickled down her fur. "Many days ago, he set out with our eldest son to get to the bottom of the noisy mischief."

Trembling, the parrot hung on her every word.

"They never returned."

"It's the humans! The humans are destroying our rainforest!" the parrot cried excitedly.

"We know that," sighed the gorilla lady. "They are already very close. We have seen it."

"We have to do something about it."

"We can't. Our territory is already mostly destroyed. Our journey ends here."

The parrot shook his head vehemently. "But it doesn't have to! We'll find a way. But first we need to get out of here!"

"But where to?" the lady gorilla complained. "This is our home. We can't leave here."

"But then you will all die!"

She nodded sadly. "It has already started. We can hardly find enough food."

"Then come with me. The jungle is big. We'll find you another territory."

"We are all sick. We are starving. Too weak for a long journey into the unknown. And surrounded by precincts that do not provide us with the habitat we need."

"What does that mean?"

The female gorilla closed her eyes wearily. "That it ends here for us."

With a tear-veiled look, the parrot swung into the air. "I will carry the word into the jungle! I will round up every animal in this forest! And I will not rest until we find a solution!"

"I wish you every success, brave parrot," whispered the lady gorilla, looking after him sorrowfully. "I'm afraid it's too late for us."

Practical application:

The animals of the jungle are caught completely unprepared by the disaster that humans are causing with their forest clearance. They had no information, could not see the threat and therefore could not prepare for it.

If they had known about the approaching humans with their machines and guns, it would have been possible to take precautions. Perhaps the gorillas would have been relocated when they were still strong and vigorous, instead of having to search for a new territory half-starved and without their wise leader.

Anyone who is poorly informed will not be able to survive for long, even in the fast-moving business world. Complete and correct information is an indispensable basis when you have to make important decisions. Act from a position of strength by always steering the fortunes of your company in a well-informed manner! Only if you know and understand the changes in the markets or your customers' expectations can you adapt your business model to new developments in your industry.

Data plays an increasingly important role in this. This fable will show you how to harness your company's data and use it profitably.

The Jungle Conference

And so the parrot flew tirelessly through the vast land. He spotted the well-camouflaged chameleon in the tall green grasses. In the dry steppes at the edge of the rainforest, he stopped the sprinting cheetah. He even ventured across the water, seeking out the dolphin in his lagoon.

On the way back into the jungle, he reported to the indignantly trumpeting elephant, informed the growling bear in his cosy den and even woke the slumbering sloth.

In the swamps, he met the jaguar, and at the edge of the forest in the bush savannah, he had a long chat with the old rhinoceros. Not far away in a river in the savannah, he finally found the hippopotamus.

In the treetops, the parrot fluttered to the playful monkeys before sharing the news with the snake dangling from a thick branch.

The parrot told them all what he had seen with his own eyes. And he brought the depressing news of the gorillas' demise. Stunned, the animals hung on his every word. They listened deep inside, and as unbelievable as the story sounded, they felt that it was the dark truth. In the end, they all agreed to meet in the heart of the jungle for a conference of animals the likes of which had not been seen for ages.

Now only one was missing: the unrestricted ruler of the forest. The king of the jungle. The most supple and powerful animal of these realms. The parrot had to pay his respects to the tiger.

From a lofty height, the parrot spotted the striped muscles creeping silently through the dense vegetation. Cautiously, he approached from above and sat down on a gnarled tree stump at a safe distance.

The tiger's sharp eyes took hold of him. The parrot felt goosebumps prickle under his colourful feathers. But he remained stoically seated. This matter was far too important!

"What brings you here?" The tiger's voice was rough and smoky. The parrot's guts tightened at the sound of it.

"We have seen the dying of the gorillas."

The king of the jungle furrowed his tabby brow. "The dying of the gorillas? You speak in riddles."

"It's the humans," the parrot blurted out. "They are destroying our rainforest. And the gorillas were the first to get it. The old silverback is dead. And the others won't survive much longer."

"Their territory is far away from here. What do I care? Every animal is responsible for itself."

"That may be. But we can only face this danger together."

"I am not a pack animal. We tigers fight only for ourselves. And always alone."

"But you are the king of this jungle. We need you to advise us." The parrot knew how to appeal to the tiger's ego. "We need your experience. Your wisdom. Your guidance. And your strength."

The tiger bared his impressive fangs vainly. "Where is the meeting taking place?"

"In the Sunny Glade in the heart of the jungle."

The tiger nodded majestically to the parrot and roamed away without a word.

The evening sun bathed the clearing in glistening orange light. The sweet scent of flowers mingled with the refreshing note of the evergreen trees. Not far away, a small brook babbled.

Satisfied, the parrot let his gaze wander through the group. They had all come. Only the dolphin was unable to leave his lagoon. The tiger was the last to appear in the Sunny Glade. With his head held high, he strode through the rows, which stepped aside reverently before his velvet paws and bowed their heads. Arriving at the centre, the king of the jungle nodded to his companions and gave the floor to the parrot.

"You all know why we are here. The end of the gorillas has affected us deeply. And so we have gathered here to find a solution that will allow us to face the threat of humans."

The jaguar bared his teeth belligerently. "We are the masters of the jungle. Humans have no business here. Let us take back what is ours."

"It's not that simple," the elephant warned. "The humans have dangerous weapons. They will not be brought to their knees in an open fight."

"But how are we supposed to protect ourselves from them then?" grumbled the bear.

"We should wait and see," thought the sloth. "Wait and save our strength. Every storm moves on at some point."

"But not the humans," the rhino found. "Their greed is boundless."

"Let's bombard them with objects from the treetops until they take flight," the monkeys giggled and rubbed their hands together thievishly.

"We won't chase them away with a few nuts," the cheetah waved off. "We have to be adaptable and come up with something better."

"Let us remember the gorillas," the elephant trumpeted respectfully. "Proud animals, loyal and strong. They could do nothing against the humans. They were taken by surprise."

"That's the core of the problem," nodded the rhino. "We only react to what the humans do. Because we have no information. Because we never know what they're going to do next."

"Information ... be adaptable ..." The hippo shook his head stubbornly. "I do not understand you. I have always lived in my river. There, the law of the strongest rules. And I am the biggest and strongest animal in my river. So I don't need information and I don't need to be adaptable." Self-confidently, the hippo let his gaze wander through the round. "Whoever stands in my way, I drown or crush. And live my life like all the other hippos before me."

Outraged voices flared up.

"But you are also part of this world ..."

"Times are changing ..."

"Without information we are doomed ..."

The thunderous bass of the elephant prevailed: "The gorillas are also incredibly strong. And yet they met an end they didn't deserve!"

Then all eyes turned to the tiger, who had not said anything so far. The king of the jungle returned the expectant looks. "I agree with the hippo," he spoke resentfully. "Do you see those claws?" He proudly stretched his massive paws aloft. "And those teeth?" He showed his imposing fangs with a roar. A frightened murmur went through the ranks. "I prefer to rely on myself. On my own strengths. I don't need information about what the humans are up to. Let them come! I will sweep them aside!"

With that, he turned on his heel and left the Sunny Glade. And the hippo followed his example.

The rest of the animals remained in the clearing. The trees were casting long shadows by now. It was getting darker. And their moods adjusted to the approaching night after the tiger's departure.

Then the bear's good-natured growl shattered the depressed mood: "Then we'll just gather the information without those two stubborn ones!"

The jaguar agreed with the bear. "Yes, let's take back the reigns of our jungle!"

"But how are we going to do it?" asked the parrot.

The rhino rubbed his pointed nose thoughtfully. "The path is long and not yet clear. But it always begins with the first step."

The monkeys groaned, "What's that supposed to mean?"

The deep, gentle voice of the elephant came across the clearing: "It means that we should not worry about the HOW until we have determined the WHAT."

The rhino nodded gratefully.

The monkeys were jumping around excitedly.

"It's about survival!", the parrot threw into the room.

"About information," the snake hissed.

"About flexibility," growled the cheetah.

"About memories," said the elephant.

"Foresight," added the rhino.

Then there was a thoughtful silence in the clearing.

"So we have a joint mission," the elephant summed up. And all the animals hung on his lips. "We are trying to gather information so that by harmonising our memories and a new foresight, we can be flexible enough to ensure the survival of us all."

A gentle breeze swept over the small clearing. It was a moment full of magic. The animals of the jungle nodded in awe.

The parrot hopped into the middle and solemnly stretched out his right wing. "So be it! Let us make a pact that commits us all to this common mission!"

One animal after the other stretched his right paw forward. "So be it!" they swore.

The inhabitants of the jungle formed a circle, touched each other with their paws and wings. And the pact was sealed.

Practical application:
What did the animals of the jungle do in this chapter? Figuratively speaking, they have made the decision to evolve into a data-driven company.

How they want to achieve their goal in concrete terms, they do not yet know at this point. But every path begins with the first step: the definition of a joint goal, a mission and a clear vision.

Only when this first step is successful, when all those involved are committed to a common goal, does a transformation stand on a secure foundation. There must be agreement on what one wants to achieve. And the goals must be packaged in a clear, understandable and, above all, tangible message that precisely describes what is to be achieved, has a motivating and inspiring effect, and is large and long-term, but at the same time realistically achievable.

This is the basis on which the journey towards a data-driven company is built.

The biggest problem for the animals of the jungle is that they have not succeeded in bringing the entire leadership level with them. With the hippopotamus and, above all, the majestic tiger, they have lost two important stakeholders whom they were unable to inspire with their plan. The transformation to a data-driven company is a profound intervention in the corporate culture and can therefore only succeed if the bottom-up cultural change is supported and actively promoted top-down by management.

Of course, it is also part of the storyline of this fable that the tiger cannot be convinced. Otherwise, it would be too easy for the animals, and the tension of the book would suffer just as much as its core messages. But it is not unrealistic in practice for there to be doubters. Statements like "We've always done it that way" or

"In our business, we can get by without data" will be encountered again and again on your journey. In the worst case, also from your management level.

Make sure to bring your leadership along from the beginning. Underline the importance of your cause in a comprehensible way: If you are poorly informed, you will not be able to survive for long in the fast-moving business world!

The Strategy of Survival

The next morning, the animals met again in the Sunny Glade.

"There is still much to discuss," the parrot fluted.

"Who remembers our joint mission?" trumpeted the elephant.

"Well, some kind of ... survival and all that stuff ...", the monkeys stammered excitedly.

The rhino sighed. "We are trying to gather information so that by harmonising our memories and a new foresight, we can be flexible enough to ensure the survival of us all."

The elephant nodded appreciatively.

The bear scratched his head thoughtfully. "But what does that mean in concrete terms?"

"I think we must now take the next step," the elephant decided. "What do we need to survive?"

"Maybe we should reverse the question," suggested the rhino. "What threatens our survival?"

"The humans!" all the animals shouted as if from one mouth.

Then there was silence.

"We have also been struggling to survive before humans invaded our jungle," the snake hissed.

The cheetah nodded: "That's right. So there must be more threats."

"Well, I find it threatening when I'm hungry and can't find anything to eat," grinned the bear.

"That's right," cried the monkeys excitedly. "Lack of food endangers our existence!"

The parrot raised his left wing in the air: "Natural disasters are a threat!"

"Yes," the animals chattered wildly. "Earthquakes and floods can really have terrible consequences!"

"And contagious diseases have already wiped out entire packs!" the jaguar added.

"Then we have found many more threats than just the humans," the elephant summarised. "Humans, food shortages, natural disasters and diseases. Let's start with that."

"The best thing to do is to split up," advised the rhino. "We form four groups and each group thinks about what information we can use to prevent these threats."

"Good idea!" the animals shouted and set to work.

The chameleon, the parrot and the jaguar discussed the human threat.

"The humans are so many, and unpredictable, and cruel," the parrot wailed in despair. "How are we going to cope with that?"

"We have to focus on our strengths," said the jaguar. "We are fast, agile, tricky and powerful. And adaptable."

"Yes, that is the key," agreed the chameleon. "We have to adapt to what humans are up to."

"Then let's list what information we need for this," suggested the parrot.

"First of all, we should know where they are."

"Where they spread to."

"What their plans are."

"What tools they have with them."

"What they have done in other jungles."

"How we can put obstacles in their way."

"Where they camp at night."

"That's good," the parrot found. "If we gather all this information, then I am confident."

At the same time, the bear was discussing with the elephant.
"We need to know as soon as possible if food is running low somewhere in the jungle," growled the bear.
"And understand the causes of it so we can fix it," added the elephant.
"It would be good to have an overview of what types of food we have available, in what quantities, and where in our jungle."
"Yes, exactly," the elephant rejoiced. "And then we should find out why there is more food in some places than others."
The bear frowned thoughtfully. "And then if we knew which animals ate how much food…"
"… then we could calculate when which foods would be in short supply."
The bear gleefully high-fived the elephant's tusk: "We make a good team!"

A little away from the clearing, the rhino, the cheetah and the monkey had a lively exchange.
"But how do we know when a natural disaster is imminent?" the monkey puzzled.
"Some animals sense an earthquake long before it happens," said the rhino.
"And volcanic eruptions too," added the cheetah.
"So we have to make sure that these animals don't just run away and leave us alone with the mess, but spread the information so that everyone can prepare," the rhino concluded.
The monkey was thrilled: "An early warning system!"
"All we need to know is when and where the disaster will strike," the cheetah muttered.
"Come, let's make a list of animals that can sense earthquakes and volcanic eruptions …"

The sloth and the snake formed the last group.

"The strength is to be found in serenity," said the sloth. "Those who rest a lot and stay calm don't get sick."

"But you are never immune to contagious diseases," the snake hissed.

"So we would have to find out where contagious diseases break out."

"Exactly, and knowing that, we can consciously avoid those regions of the jungle."

"This way we can sidestep and wipe out any disease!"

The animals of the jungle met again in their clearing to share the results of the four groups. They were excited and enthusiastic.

"Now each of us knows the information we need to gather in order to achieve our goals," the elephant summarised. "Each one of you now has the task of gathering this information and sharing it with the others. This is how we ensure our survival."

The animals set off into their territory. And they began to gather information.

Practical application:
Successful data use needs a common strategy and direction. In the previous chapter we have already seen that a strategy needs clearly named and mutually agreed goals.

To concretise a good data strategy, it is still necessary to break down these goals into more tangible sub-goals.

For example, do you want to pursue the goal of maintaining your competitiveness as a data-driven company?

Various sub-goals can be derived from this, for example cost reduction, turnover increase, an increase in profit margins, or the development of new products or services.

The specific sub-goals help you to think more deeply about what data you need to achieve your goals.

Feel free to involve your colleagues in this process, for example in the form of interactive breakout sessions. This way, those involved identify with the jointly developed sub-goals right from the start, and more heads usually lead to more creativity and foresight.

Ultimately, it is a matter of deriving a concrete action plan from the rough goals that is precise, task-oriented and ideally also measurable.

You know your business goals best. What data-related goals can you derive from them? How can you measure their achievement quantitatively and qualitatively?

The Magic of the Forest

The animals began to gather information day by day. The birds observed the movements of the humans from their lofty heights. The predatory cats exchanged information about where they could snatch prey. Unexpected vibrations of the earth were communicated immediately. And the animals reported any kind of illness.

But soon their heads were spinning.

Whining, the parrot sat down on the tip of the rhino's nose and gave vent to his disappointment. "I imagined it totally different."

"Yeah, me too."

"Somehow it works ..."

"... and yet somehow not," replied the rhinoceros.

"But what are we doing wrong?"

The rhinoceros thought for a long time before answering: "Our plan is good. I am convinced of that. However, it is a lot of work to gather all this information. And to analyse it."

"That's right. I'd be interested to hear what the others think about it."

"Then fly out once more, brave parrot, and gather the animals. It seems to me that another consultation in the Sunny Glade is needed."

And again the animals followed the parrot's call. They all gathered in the Sunny Glade in the heart of the forest. Even the tiger had come because he was curious to see how the scheme worked. And there was no end to the moaning and complaining.

"I am constantly informed where the cheetah and the jaguar are snatching fat prey!"

"And I only ever hear about drinking places that are so far away from my territory that I would have died of thirst before I got there."

"I'm already getting sick of all the diseases I hear about all day long!"

"Do you know what makes me sick? All this rushing around! I'm more busy gathering information than food!"

"That's right," the sloth nodded eagerly. "That's terrible. Such a hassle! You don't get to do anything anymore. Not even a good nap!"

"And then there's the passing on of the information," groaned the snake. "I'm already hoarse from all the hissing and whispering!"

"And by the time the information reaches me, it's so old that it doesn't help me anymore."

The tiger smiled knowingly. "I told you right away. Rely on your own strength. And forget all that frippery!" And with these words he trotted off disinterestedly, leaving the animals of the jungle in their misery.

A disillusioned silence filled the Sunny Glade. The parrot beat his brightly coloured wings over his eyes in bitterness. *Our plan has failed,* he thought dejectedly.

"I think the tiger is wrong!" the elephant thundered in a firm voice. "Do you really want to discard all the great ideas right away just because the beginning is a bit bumpy?"

The other animals sheepishly avoided the admonishing look of his wise eyes.

The rhino cleared his throat. "Then I guess we should face the challenges."

"If I understand it correctly, we have three problems," the elephant summarised. "It takes too much time and effort to collect the information. It reaches those who need it too late. And we get too much information that we don't need at all. Is that correct?"

The animals nodded in agreement. And they began to ponder how to solve this. They debated until darkness descended on the Sunny Glade. But they found no way out.

It was already dark when the parrot disappointedly ended the meeting. They had failed. There was no solution to their plight. But they didn't want to just carry on like this either.

Suddenly, an enchanting light illuminated the Sunny Glade, which was as brilliantly white as they had ever seen it. But so warm that it still didn't hurt their eyes.

Straining, the animals stared in the direction of the light, but they could see nothing. Only the soft singing of bright voices could they hear, as pure and clear as the gentle morning dew.

Then the unicorn stepped into the clearing and flowers blossomed around her hooves. The animals of the forest stared in amazement at the legendary mythical creature, which they all thought was a fairy tale.

With lithe steps, the sparkling creature ran into the centre of the clearing. The pointed horn flashed in the moonlight. The good-natured eyes regarded the reverent animals, and they all bowed their heads before the majestic figure.

"I have heard of your intention." The gentle voice enchanted the animals and warmed their souls and hearts. "It shows extraordinary courage to go out and change the world. And so I make you a gift of the magic of nature."

In a sublime manner, the unicorn lowered her head and touched the mossy ground of the forest with her horn. And the unicorn's magic flowed into the roots of the jungle.

The plants began to interconnect. Magic wove invisible threads in the depths of the earth. The plants of the primeval forest became one.

"Now you are linked to the roots of the earth. Quick as the wind, the plants will grasp the information. And spread it like wildfire."

Proudly, the unicorn nodded one last time to the grateful animals. And before they awoke from their reverent trance, she was gone.

The elephant swallowed to dispel the unicorn's spell from his fogged senses. "Then let's get going!" he trumpeted with a broad smile. And the animals of the jungle burst into cheers.

Practical application:

The challenge of the animals in this chapter is not uncommon: too high a degree of manual processes, and an aimless distribution of information in boundless abundance.

The core message of these experiences is as clear as it is obvious.

You should not aimlessly distribute information to all colleagues without checking its relevance. The magic phrase is: target group orientation. It is important that everyone has the opportunity to get the information they need. But if you indiscriminately flood the entire company with data, it is hard to see the forest for the trees - and the really important information gets lost and is not used.

Also try to avoid manual processes as much as possible. Don't limit your considerations to the nightly data flows that likely already exist in every company. Look for manual data preparations where ambitious users download data from reports or from the data warehouse to process them manually in applications such as Access or Excel. Always ask yourself what the goal of the manual processes is, and if they are done regularly, check whether they can be automated.

A high level of automation is the key to efficiency and the distributed use of data that characterises a data-driven company.

Fortunately, you don't need a magic unicorn to master these challenges. There are many sophisticated tools on the market that can efficiently and qualitatively help you automate your data flows and also provide your users with sound and reusable ways to prepare data and develop dashboards and reports on their own.

Take advantage of these offers - they are the foundation on which a data-driven company is built.

Where are the recurring manual efforts hidden in your company where there is still room for optimisation?

The Visual Revolution

Thrilled, the animals realised what an incredible gift the unicorn had given them. The inhabitants of the jungle ran through the undergrowth with broad grins.

"It's madness," the bear growled, his eyes twinkling. "As soon as I lick honey somewhere, the trees get it and transmit the information through their roots."

The sloth could not believe his luck. "I finally have time for a long nap again. And the branches seem to sense where I can take a safe nap and pass this information on immediately."

The parrot also fluttered happily above the treetops and watched contentedly as the magic of nature unfolded its full effect. Everything was suddenly so simple, so smooth, so magical. "And I was about to submit to fate. The elephant was right! One must never give up!" Curiously, he looked at the leaves in the treetops, which were constantly changing their colours. In magnificent patterns, they represented the information collected and distributed via the networked root system of the primeval forest.

One day, the jaguar was roaming through the jungle. It was a hot morning. The scorching sun burned mercilessly from the sky. Tired, he dragged himself from shade to shade. Many of the usual drinking places had already dried up. The powerful animal craved water.

Finally, he found a deserted waterhole a little way off in a clearing. With a scrutinizing look the jaguar looked up at the treetops. The leaves sparkled down at him in red colours. "At last!" he growled in relief. "That's the signal that directs me to this drinking spot." Quickly he stuck his muzzle into the cool water and greedily slurped the refreshing water down his throat. It tasted a little brackish, but the thirst quencher was still good.

When the jaguar awoke the next morning, he groaned painfully. His stomach cramped up and tormented him. He no longer understood the world. *It couldn't have been the water. After all, our information system led me to this watering hole. But what was it then?*

The jaguar tried to get up, but he couldn't. He writhed in pain.

By chance, the sloth came along and watched him curiously. "Say, jaguar, you're not going to become a sloth too, are you?"

"A sloth? Me?"

"Well, even I don't lie around as much as you do."

The jaguar showed his fangs and moaned: "Be glad I can't get up. I'd love to teach you some manners."

"What happened?"

"I don't know. As such, I only drank from the water over there. Since then I've had terrible stomach pains."

The sloth frowned. "From that water?"

"Yes, of course."

"Well, that doesn't surprise me then. The trees have marked the watering hole in red."

"Well, of course, to emphasise that it's a particularly good watering hole."

"But red is a warning, isn't it?" asked the sloth.

"Well, that doesn't sound very logical," groaned the jaguar.

"Yellow leaves highlight the really good water points."

By chance, the parrot flew past. "You two look so cosy together. I'm going to lie down with you too."

"We are not lying down," growled the jaguar irritably. "We are suffering! Well, I am, at least."

"Why are you suffering?"

"I drank from the watering hole there."

The parrot was startled. "But didn't you see the warning in the treetops? Red is a clear warning!"

"That's what I said," the sloth grinned contentedly.

"I only drink from water points marked green. They are safe!" the parrot fluted.

"Why green? Yellow are the really good ones!"

"Yellow? I wouldn't even clean my beak in that!"

Then it dawned on the parrot. Sighing, he slapped his colourful wing on his forehead and called out: "Excuse me, please! Urgent business! We'll meet tomorrow, when the sun is at its highest, in the Sunny Glade!"

And the parrot set off to gather the animals in the clearing one more time.

"Why are we here again?" the bear brooded. "Everything is going well."

"Nothing is going well at all," the parrot announced in a reproachful voice. "The unicorn has given us an incomparable gift and we are too stupid to use it properly."

Protesting murmurs bubbled in the Sunny Glade. The animals did not agree with this harsh statement.

"Well, I use the information of the forest day by day." The bear grinned dreamily. "And the honey has never tasted better."

Shaking his head, the parrot tucked his wings into his hips. "Which of you can tell me what pattern the treetops display to warn us of an approaching storm?"

The animals busily stretched their paws, claws and hooves into the air.

"Me!"

"Me!"

"Me!" they shouted with conviction.

"Then tell me," demanded the parrot.

Filled with fervent conviction, all the animals of the forest roared wildly.

"A square!"

"A circle!"

"A triangle!"

"Stripes!"

"You have one more try." The parrot had decided to put his finger even deeper into the wound. "Which of you can tell me what colour the leaves use to warn us of impending danger?"

A second time, the animals eagerly stretched their paws upwards.

"Me!"

"Me!"

"Me!" they shouted with conviction.

"Then tell me," the parrot demanded again.

And the animals almost rolled over to be the first to give the right answer.

"Green!"

"Blue!"

"Red!"

"Yellow!"

"Pink!"

"Black!"

"Orange!"

The parrot looked sternly at the shaken group: "Easy to prove!"

It was the rhino that regained his composure first. "Everyone interpreted the information in their own way!" he stammered in shock.

The elephant dug his tusks into the ground in shame. "We don't have any standards that determine the meaning of the information."

"We have to change that quickly before anything more happens than a spoiled stomach!" cried the cheetah excitedly.

Then the heavy-breathing hippo broke through the thicket, dragging the caiman's lifeless body behind it. Blood gushed from two deep wounds in the green scaly skin.

"What happened?" the parrot stammered.

"The humans!" the hippo gasped. "It was the humans!"

"Is he still alive?"

"He was earlier. He was floating unconscious in the river."

The animals hurriedly examined the caiman. But his brave heart was no longer beating.

"Oh no," sobbed the parrot. "Not again! Please, please don't!"

"How could this happen?" asked the chalky elephant.

"Yesterday he was still telling me that he can finally move along the riverbank without fear. Because the treetops show him where the humans have not spread yet." Reproachfully, the hippopotamus let his sparking eyes wander around. "There you see what you get out of your new ideas!" And with a grim face, the hippo stomped off.

Devoutly, the animals of the jungle buried the heavy body of the caiman in a starry night. And when their bitter tears had dried up, they gave meaning to the colourful spectacle of the jungle. Tirelessly they matched colours and patterns and carved the results into an ancient rock at the edge of the clearing so that they would endure forever. And they hoped that this measure would prevent further suffering.

Practical application:
It is of immense importance to provide high-quality data.

And yet this data is worth nothing if it cannot be interpreted correctly. They can even be dangerous if you draw the wrong conclusions from them in a misguided belief. The jaguar had to learn this painfully first-hand. And the caiman even dramatically paid for his misinterpretations with his life.

At the end of this chapter, the animals of the jungle have worked out common visualisation standards. They have recorded a notation of how they want to present information and how the information presented is to be interpreted.

Where treetops work with patterns, data and analytics teams use modern chart types to give meaning to data. Visual representations in the form of charts, maps or graphs are able to highlight important trends in a tangible way.

But the visualisation of information is not as easy as it seems. Your visualisation standards should therefore include clear recommendations as to which form of presentation enables the best possible insight in which case, and define clear rules as to how you want to convey a precise and undistorted message in an appealing way.

And also in a data-driven company, it is advisable to agree on the meaning of colours. What colour do negative and positive deviations get? How are planned values distinguished from actual values?

The animals' final trick was not simply to agree on the visualisation standards verbally. No, the animals put the defined standards in writing. A helpful reference book for the future to avoid any misunderstandings.

Now the inhabitants of the jungle are armed to make consistent use of the high-quality data. Don't hesitate and give meaning to your data too.

Summary Part 1

In the face of threats to their habitat, the animals of the forest have set the first course for a data-driven jungle.

They have responded to the disruption of their changing environment and realised that they cannot survive without better information.

As a result of this insight, they defined a clear objective, which they then broke down into actionable sub-goals.

The gift of automation and the definition of common visualisation standards have finally enabled them to extract and interpret information. The first step towards a data-driven jungle.

Part 2

… in which the animals of the forest build a strong foundation on which the development of a data culture in their jungle is possible.

The Dolphin´s Academy

With a grim face, the orangutan swung through the treetops. His stomach growled. He was tired. And he simply could not understand how the forest had changed so quickly.

He was a clever animal. The orangutan knew every tree in his several square kilometres of territory by name. He had always known which leaves could be eaten, which plants had healing powers, and when which fruit from which tree was particularly ripe and tasty. Yes, there had been no need to worry about him. Until the world started to go crazy from one day to the next …

Desperately, the tapir dragged his trunk over the damp earth. He was confused. Stability was the most important thing to him. And for many years he had been the only one who knew about these great feeding places on the riverbank. For a few weeks, however, it had been like a jinx. His most secret hiding places were being robbed by voracious competitors. The tapir could not explain it. How did everyone suddenly seem to know where to find the best food? When no one had ever been able to outdo his fine nose …

Annoyed, the tapir tramped through the undergrowth.

"What a jinx this is!" he cursed. "As if the whole world had conspired against me …"

"I have to agree with you," a bright voice suddenly sounded. Rapidly, the orangutan swung down on a vine and shook his head. "Nothing is the way it was."

"But why?" asked the tapir.

"I don't know," the orangutan whined. "But I'm glad that others feel the same way."

"I'd be interested to know what's going on."

"Have you also seen how the trees change the colours of their leaves all at once?"

"I don't see so well," mused the tapir. "But now that you mention it ... it's spooky, don't you think?"

"Yes. Spooky. And strange. Why would the leaves change colours?"

"Colours ... If that was my only concern."

The orangutan stared at him reproachfully and raised his index finger in the air. "Did you know that I can recognise hundreds of plants just by the green hue of their leaves? That's how I choose my meals. Only the best for the orangutan!"

"And then what happens?"

"The forest has gone crazy for a fortnight, my friend! I spy a tasty leaf, swing over there like a gymnastics champion, just about to take a bite ... then the leaf changes colour from one second to the next!"

"So what? Then take a bite anyway."

The orangutan tapped his forehead wildly. "Are you crazy? Just bite into it? Who knows what I'll eat then?"

"You've got problems ..." the tapir muttered with a despondent shake of his head. "What am I supposed to say? I can't find any good food anymore. Because the best morsels are constantly being snatched away from under my nose. It's like someone just knows everything. Everything!"

"We can't go on like this!" the orangutan exclaimed.

"Yes, we have to do something about it."

"But against what?"

"That's what we need to find out!"

Searching, the mismatched pair roamed through the jungle. The tapir and the orangutan moved further away from their territory than ever before in their lives.

Until finally, one beautiful evening, they stood in a dreamlike clearing. The glowing red sun bathed the quiet spot of earth in a glistening orange. They immediately felt the mysterious magic emanating from this place.

"Look, here!" the orangutan pointed with his mouth wide open.

"What is that supposed to be? A rock?"

"Yes, but someone wrote in here."

"It says something about patterns. And colours. What does it all mean?"

All at once, a small parrot settled on the rock and gawked questioningly at the tapir and the orangutan. "We didn't think of you," he murmured, nodding. "Good that you are here ..."

"What's going on?"

"What does it all mean?"

"Sit down," said the parrot. "I will tell you the most incredible story of this jungle ..."

When the parrot had finished, the orangutan and the tapir looked at him with wide eyes.

"So that's the solution to the riddle ..."

"I would never have thought of that!"

But their astonishment quickly gave way to growing concern.

"If this information is available to some animals but not to us ..." the orangutan mused.

"... then we'll starve to death because we won't find any more food!" the tapir added grimly.

"The animals are all very familiar with it already!"

"We'll never be able to make up this deficit!"

The parrot frowned worriedly. "You are right, but it was never meant to be like this. We were always concerned about all the animals of the jungle. We wanted to create a better world for everyone, not for someone to starve because of us."

"Then you shouldn't have forgotten us!" the orangutan rumbled.

The parrot felt sorry for the two of them. The images of the caiman's mortal wounds were still too burnt into his brain to underestimate the fatal consequences of inexperience. Feverishly, he searched for a solution.

"We have to find a way to give all the animals of the jungle access to our project ..."

The tapir and the orangutan nodded eagerly.

"... and there must be a way to catch up by explaining everything in deep detail to newcomers."

"But in doing so, we should not be distracted by other everyday things," the orangutan reflected.

"And it has to be quick," the tapir thought.

"Yes," said the parrot. "But who can explain so much information well?"

"It must be a clever animal," exclaimed the orangutan, "if it is to excel in all aspects."

"And it has to be a friendly mate who makes you feel comfortable and happy to learn."

Thoughtfully, the parrot put his colourful wing to the tip of his beak. "So we are looking for a clever and friendly animal that lives somewhat secluded in an environment conducive to learning."

The three thought about this profile for a moment.

"The Dolphin's Lagoon!" they all blurted out at once.

And so the parrot fluttered the long way to the Dolphin's Lagoon.

"Parrot, good to see you," the dolphin greeted the rare visitor. "How can I help you?"

"Do you remember our bold plan to gather information?"

"Of course," the dolphin smiled. "Unfortunately, I am not able to attend your meetings in the Sunny Glade because I cannot leave the lagoon. But I follow your project with great interest. And I have felt the changes in the roots of the forest all the way into the waves of my lagoon."

"Would you like to be part of our venture?"

The dolphin looked at the parrot in amazement. "How is that supposed to work? I am not as free and unbound as you and cannot leave my element to confer with you."

Then the parrot told about the troubles of the tapir and the orangutan.

The dolphin's eyes lit up: "We could start an academy for the animals of the jungle here in my lagoon!"

The parrot smiled when he saw the enthusiasm: "That would be wonderful!"

The dolphin bowed solemnly. "I would be honoured to teach the animals the secrets of our forest."

Practical application:

An emerging data culture is changing the everyday life of many colleagues - and some employees will find this change challenging.

It is easy to get the frontrunners excited about your project. They swim along on the first wave, are curious and eager to learn, good pilots for new ideas and the desired cultural change.

And in the process, the supporters of stability and habit fall by the wayside. How do you engage those who don't embrace change from the start, who can't yet grasp the added value, and who cling to long-established but familiar and tried-and-tested processes?

In order to become data-driven, all those involved must develop a basic understanding step by step. What is possible with data? Why is this change necessary? What added value can it bring? What is the role of the individual in this? And how can they swim along on the wave without losing their connection?

But understanding alone will not make you data-driven. A second essential building block is missing: skills. Colleagues must have the opportunity to learn how to profitably use the tools, reports and information on offer.

The combination of shared understanding and the necessary skills - data literacy - are the foundations of data culture. Culture change cannot be commanded or forced. It must be carefully sown, allowed to grow and mature, and consistently reaped.

It is important to create data literacy offerings that are appropriate for the target group. Offer basic courses for beginners, but also give experienced users the chance to develop their data skills and get even more value from their data. Think not only about technology, but also about methodological competence or the teaching of standards.

If your employees develop both an understanding of the potential and the necessary implementation skills, your company will be well-equipped to generate great added value from your data.

Which data literacy target groups do you see in your company? What do these target groups need to learn in your academy to better integrate data into their daily work processes? How can your training offers create tangible added value for your colleagues?

The Elephant's Law

With a contorted mouth, the parrot held his motley belly: "My goodness. I'm bursting!" But the information in the treetops told him without doubt that the feeding was not yet finished. "Oh my goodness, this can't be happening!"

The parrot frowned thoughtfully. "What if the information is not correct at all?" he murmured. "That would be fatal. At some point I'll really burst. And that's only because the roots made a mistake!"

Immediately he pushed his food aside, sat down on a branch and suspiciously observed the many helpful tips displayed in the treetops.

Suddenly he heard an indignant cry. "Damn it, this can't be happening! Not again! Such a fu ..."

"There, there," the parrot placated. "We won't swear after all."

"These branches ... I can't stand them!" cried the sloth indignantly. "They're driving me crazy."

Lazily, the parrot made his way to the next branch, where the sloth, marked with dark circles under his eyes, dangled upside down.

"What's got you all riled up?"

Grimly, the sloth looked at the branches. "They won't let me sleep," he whined, "they keep waking me up again!"

The parrot mused. *I must eat too much, the sloth must not sleep. What's going on? How is it all connected? The whole jungle is going crazy!*

The branches and trees trembled. A loud rustling snapped him out of his thoughts. The parrot looked around in panic. Then the elephant thundered out of the thicket. His tusks gleamed in the midday sun. His eyes were huge. The trunk quivered.

"Quick, we have to get out of here!"

The parrot's heart skipped a beat. *When the elephant is scared, it looks really bad!*

"What happened? Why the rush?" asked the sloth, whose tiredness had suddenly vanished.

"Humans!" the elephant growled.

The sloth deftly slid off his branch and sat on the elephant's back. The parrot swung into the air.

The elephant immediately stomped off. "That way!"

"I didn't know ... that the humans ... had already advanced so far," the parrot stammered between his hasty breaths.

The elephant's expression became deadly serious. "Neither did I. The jungle should have warned us much earlier!"

They quickly looked up into the treetops. And what they saw there made their blood run cold.

"They're getting closer!" screeched the sloth.

Hastily, the elephant looked around. "This way! We can hide there!"

They hurried towards a gigantic bush, a wall of vines and ferns big enough to hide even a full-grown elephant.

Trembling, they cowered in their hiding place, trying to calm their ragged breathing. And listened. In the distance they heard footsteps rustling in the grass. Cautiously they peeked through the branches.

"Ha, ha, ha!" echoed through the jungle.

Puzzled, the elephant looked at the sloth and the parrot.

"They'll be surprised!"

Then the parrot's sharp eyes caught sight of the hairy creatures grinning as they romped through the forest. "They're in for a treat!"

Enraged, the elephant rumbled out of hiding and reared up with his imposing stature in front of the seven monkeys, who stared at him, giggling inanely. "Haha, the elephant seems to be a taxi. He's carrying a sloth around on his back!"

"You're about to stop laughing!" the elephant rumbled and lowered his tusks threateningly. The giggling stopped instantly. "What do you think you are doing here?"

"Have fun. What else?"

The elephant eyed the monkeys, who wore ragged and tattered human shoes on their feet. "I'm about to enjoy spanking you simpletons!"

"Just join in," the monkeys suggested. "It's really entertaining to keep the whole jungle on its toes."

"I ... don't understand ...", the sloth pondered.

"We first noticed it when we were eating," the monkeys explained. "When you pretend to eat, but you're just pretending, it confuses our great information system. The snake almost burst, he was eating so much because the treetops kept telling him to eat more."

"You're deliberately confusing our information?" the parrot cried indignantly, thrusting his wings to his hips.

"Of course, it's great fun. And it's very simple. Just look at the rings around the sloth's eyes!"

"That was you as well?" sighed the sloth.

The gleeful giggling of the monkeys was answer enough.

"And with the shoes, you have made us believe that humans are on their way here," the elephant concluded.

"Of course. Oh, how you fled in panic!"

"I'll give you a reason to flee in a minute!" grumbled the elephant. "But on the other hand, you have uncovered an important loophole in our plan by your outrageous mischief."

"But what are we supposed to do about it?" the parrot whined. "If you can influence the quality of information so easily, surely we can never trust our jungle again!"

"Yes we can," said the elephant. "I have an idea." Turning inward, he set off for the Dolphin's Lagoon. And the other animals followed him.

"Hello, dolphin," greeted the pachyderm. "How's your academy going?"

"Very good, we have many interested visitors. How can I help you? I am not sure whether I can teach you anything new."

Then the elephant told him what they had found out in the jungle. The monkeys squirmed under the reproachful gaze of the dolphin.

"This is not good. We should have thought about that."

"Yes, you never stop learning," agreed the elephant. "But I have an idea."

"I'm very excited."

"The core of the problem is that the information is automatic."

"But that's good, it's less work that way!" the sloth immediately interrupted him.

"It is, but no one is responsible for ensuring the accuracy of the information."

The animals were silent. Tensely they hung on the elephant's lips.

"You can confuse the automatisms because there is no testing. And as soon as one of us has a bad experience because of jokers like our monkeys here, confidence in the plan goes down."

"But how can we change that?"

"By establishing clear responsibilities," the elephant explained in a firm voice.

"And that's supposed to work?" the parrot asked skeptically.

"Who knows the most about food?"

The animals thought for a moment. "The bear is the most greedy eater."

"Then the bear is our food expert. And thus he should also be responsible for ensuring the quality of information on this topic."

The animals nodded eagerly.

"And who knows the movements of humans best?"

"The vultures or the eagles. They see the most from high in the air."

"Well then, who better to check the information on the humans?"

The animals nodded more and more.

"And who knows best about sleeping?"

The sloth almost toppled over, so hastily did he raise his arm in the air.

"You see?" spoke the elephant. "It's very simple."

"A great idea," the dolphin squeaked gleefully. "How can I help you?"

"We lay down the structures right away and describe what exactly you have to do if you are responsible for a piece of information. It has to be clear to everyone what they have to do and what the procedures are."

"But how do we make sure that everyone exercises it carefully?"

"We need some kind of body to monitor quality and set standards and procedures," the elephant reflected.

"And who will lead this body?"

"Me!" decided the elephant with his head proudly held high.

"Then he is ... our governor, so to speak," the monkeys stammered respectfully.

"In a manner of speaking, yes!"

The dolphin clapped excitedly. "I will immediately prepare a new training in our academy so that we can instruct all those responsible in the best possible way!"

"Thank you very much!" the elephant replied and indicated a bow. Then he strutted off with broad shoulders.

Practical application:

When many stakeholders collaborate based on data, the complexity of a company's data landscape requires common rules and roles.

The elephant has taken up this issue and introduced an initial governance model for the jungle. This is the basis for anchoring good, structured governance of work with data in the organisation. And that is the foundation for trust in data quality.

Data governance can be as complex and detailed as desired, with numerous facets and focal points. In any case, however, it should start with a clear definition of roles and responsibilities. Who is responsible for monitoring the automatisms? Who validates the correctness of the data content? What is the process if someone uncovers data quality problems? These processes should then be embedded in the overall IT governance process landscape, for example by linking seamlessly to your organisation's support processes.

In many companies, the technical managers in the data and analytics teams and the data stewards, who are rather on the business side, share the responsibilities for checking and ensuring the correctness, completeness, consistency and uniformity of data.

In larger organisations, as the elephant suggested, it is quite common to establish committees and steering groups that take care of the compliance and further development of the defined roles, standards and structures.

It is important that the term "governance" is not perceived as a burden in your company. Target-oriented governance should be lean and focus on making a clear contribution to the company's goals through target-oriented rules and processes, rather than blocking them with unnecessary bureaucracy.

A good example of (too) strict data governance is the "need to know" principle, where access to data is only granted to those who can prove that they need it and for what purpose. Is it not more conducive to the flourishing of a data culture to turn the tables and establish a principle of right to information? In this alternative principle, access to company data is fundamentally granted to all employees as long as it is not sensitive or personal data.

What examples of too narrowly tailored data governance do you know from your company? How could these aspects be designed in a more target-oriented way?

The Parrot's Gospel

"Elephant, you are a fox!" said the parrot with shining eyes and tapped the pachyderm on the mighty shoulder with his tiny wing.

"A fox?" rumbled the elephant, puzzled. "Such a small, puny, red, bushy thing?" He wrinkled his trunk. "I don't think so ..."

"But foxes are very clever."

"Elephants as well!"

The elephant's ideas were a big step forward. Both friends were aware of this.

"We are on the right track."

They stared dreamily up into the treetops of the jungle with satisfied faces. A comfortable silence settled over the jungle. There was a smell of damp grass. The leaves rustled. And suddenly their breath caught.

"Did you see that too?" the elephant stammered.

"Yes," croaked the parrot.

Shocked, they stared at the orange patterns. There was no doubt.

"The humans are on the move!"

The parrot swung into the air. "I have to see this on the spot."

The elephant stared after him for a long time.

The parrot watched the activities of the humans from a dense treetop. They quickly spread out, moved in with heavy equipment, cut down trees, destroyed precious habitat. Tears ran down the colourful plumage. Then he had seen enough.

With a grim face, he rose into the air. His rage was not only directed against the humans, but also against the ignorant who did nothing against them.

He found the tiger at the edge of the jungle, whispering with the stubborn hippo. Angrily, the parrot settled down between the two and thrust his wings reproachfully into his hips.

"Are you satisfied now?" he barked at them disrespectfully. And immediately looked into the razor-sharp fangs of the majestic tiger. The blood froze in his veins. But this matter was too important to surrender to his fate, trembling with fear.

"There you see what you have achieved with your pointless information," said the hippo with a sneer. "Nothing!"

"Humans are spreading and you are not in a position to stop it," the tiger agreed with the ignorant hippo.

"Maybe we would be if we all stuck together," the parrot scolded fearlessly. His anger gave him unexpected bravery. One swipe of the tiger´s paw and he would be nothing but a featherless bloodstain in the green landscape.

"We will preserve our habitats," the tiger growled grimly, nodding confidently at the hippo. "Alone, on our own, and without your newfangled mumbo-jumbo!"

"And what about our habitats?"

"That's your problem!"

"We can tell you exactly where the humans are spreading out, where there are how many humans." The parrot did not give up. "You could hit them at their weak points. Maybe we can drive them away that way."

"I don't need any weak points." The tiger looked proudly at his imposing muscles and deadly claws. "I can take them on whenever and wherever I want."

"Then what are you waiting for?" roared the parrot.

"On the right moment, and on them threatening MY habitat."

"Selfish muscleman!" the parrot cursed as he looked down from high in the air at the jungle that lay so calm, green and innocent below him, yet in great danger. "We would be able to hand you the key to defend our jungle. And you smug idiot just ignore it!"

Tired, he sat down on a branch. How could one convince the tiger? He was far superior to them all in strength and savageness. Only the pressure of the community could possibly bring him to his senses. *But we are too few,* thought the parrot.

That's when the image of the tapir and the orangutan popped up in his mind's eye. They had not been involved from the beginning, but they had become a committed part of their community. *How many more of them are out there?* the parrot mused. *We need more supporters! An alliance of the jungle! Maybe that's the way we can convince even the tiger in the end!*

And once more the tireless parrot took off. He flew into the southern swamps of the jungle, fluttered over the tall trees of the north, swung his wings through the reddish evening light in the west and passed over the refreshing morning sky with the hummingbirds in the east. And everywhere he loudly spread the news of the power of information like a preacher proclaims the gospel.

"There are so many things to discover up there in the treetops," he enthused, lilting. "Help in finding food, warning of danger! There are no limits to the information." Like a market crier, the parrot advertised their project: "Don't lag behind the other animals! Join in, try it out, get excited! You won't regret it. Believe me!"

And he had the right answer to every question. "Of course, you have to learn a lot of new things, I admit. But you all know the dolphin in the old lagoon. He even founded his own academy for you. Believe me! There you will all benefit from his wisdom. He will teach you what you need to know. And then you can start with focused competence. Believe me!"

Of course, there were also doubters. But the elephant had paved the way for them all to convert these heretics. "You have concerns that the information is not correct? We had those too. But your worries are unfounded. For there are clear roles and responsibilities. Quality is always monitored. And the best part is: You can even join in and take responsibility yourself! Visit the dolphin in his lagoon and ask for the role model. He will explain everything to you in more detail. And then look for the elephant. If you can convince him of your strengths, he will quickly assign you an exciting role. It works like clockwork! Believe me!"

And when the parrot had finished his flight through the remotest corners of the jungle and sat down exhausted on a branch near the Dolphin´s Lagoon, he sighed contentedly when he saw the many animals marching through the dense grasses deep below him and making a pilgrimage to the Dolphin´s Academy.

Practical application:
The motto "Do good and talk about it" (Georg-Volkmar Graf Zedtwitz-Arnim) cannot only be used for public relations. It also hits the nail on the head for your data and analytics strategy.

The best governance concept will not help you if nobody knows it and thus it is not followed by the stakeholders.

The best data strategy will fizzle out if it is not lived in the company.

Who will attend a data academy they have never heard of?

You need comrades-in-arms, you have to convince interested parties of new ideas and sell the benefits of change in a practical and value-added way.

Communication is an immensely important key to the successful development of a sustainable data culture. Spark the interest, create an understanding of the new possibilities, get the doubting colleagues to understand the added value of data initiatives. Ensure that the message reaches the colleagues you want to convince through constant and targeted communication. Be creative about the best way and medium to reach your target groups.

A change in the data culture is only possible if you do not force the desired development on those involved, but by winning over fellow campaigners out of conviction!

How can you communicate the benefits in your company using the most concrete examples possible?

The Harmony of the Rhino

The rhino leisurely lowered his grey head and ate a tuft of grass. Satisfied, he began to chew while observing the surroundings. Nature offered an impressive spectacle. Colourful plants lined the edge of the jungle where it bordered the grassy savannah that the rhino called home. The blades of grass swayed in the gentle wind.

Thoughtfully, the rhino observed the information in the distant treetops. Then he frowned. There had been times when even an ardent advocate like the rhinoceros had doubts about the quality. But since the elephant had risen to become the governor of information, everything was going in the right direction.

Still, it was strange at times. *I am standing here in the middle of the savannah and the trees tell me something about poisonous animals approaching and warn me about the water quality in the jungle.* The rhino was not aware of any example where poisonous dart frogs or snakes had ventured out of the jungle. Not even old stories existed about this. And that the water quality suffered from the machinations of humans was understandable. But it was highly unlikely that this was true for the entire jungle. The rhino continued to chew. And he pondered.

Who knows what information nature consults, he mused. *With the clear responsibilities, we have made a big step forward. But some things are still not so clear to me.* He looked at the jungle, lying there so still and peaceful. And he became aware of the infinite size of the jungle, which one simply could not comprehend.

If we really want to understand what's going on in the jungle, we have to be able to make comparisons, the rhino continued to ponder, smacking his lips. *What is happening in the east? How are humans affecting the west? Are there perhaps different developments in the south? What dangers lurk in the north?*

"Somehow the grass here tastes better in spring than in summer," the rhino murmured, smacking his lips.

And in that moment of grass-chewing harmony, the rhino noticed what he had been missing all along: the harmony of information. What was a normal development in the north could trigger warning signals and panic in the animals in the south. The individual pieces of the puzzle were good and helpful, but they did not fit together.

"Spring and summer!" Sighing, the rhino set his massive body in motion. "It's time to pay the elephant a visit."

The elephant watched with delight the busy traffic flowing from the academy in the Dolphin's Lagoon back to the animals' territories.

A rustling in the thicket caught his attention. Suspiciously, he raised an eyebrow and stared at the tall, thick grass. Something large and heavy was approaching. The pachyderm lowered his head slightly to greet a potential enemy with his impressive tusks.

Exhausted, the rhino burst out of the bushes. "My old friend and governor, how long it's been since we've seen each other!"

The elephant immediately relaxed. "Yes, this is truly a nice surprise! What brings you here to the depths of the jungle?"

"Thoughts, my friend. Thoughts I can't make sense of yet."

Interested, the elephant settled on the sprawling rump and looked at the rhino expectantly. "Well, don't keep me in suspense."

"So you really think we've forgotten something?"

"Yes and no," replied the rhino. "The information is there. And it's good. But something doesn't add up yet."

"I can't quite grasp that yet."

"Look. I'll explain with an example." The rhino rubbed the tip of his nose excitedly. "I walked a lot through the jungle on the way here to find you. And in the process I noticed inconsistencies that we should deal with."

"What kind of inconsistencies?"

"When I drank from a lake in the south, the pool in the treetops was touted as a very watery lake. But in the north, I tell you, it would have been no more than a small pond. Different standards apply there."

"Different standards you say?"

"Yes. Nature interprets the information differently in different regions, depending on the circumstances."

"But ..." the elephant stammered. "But how are we supposed to answer the question, for example, where the best water sources are?"

"My opinion exactly, my friend! That is the crucial question."

"Oh dear," wailed the elephant. "This is not good!"

"And it goes even further. Places are only the tip of the iceberg. The seasons mix things up even more. My grass tastes different in spring than in autumn. And not only that, it's more nutritious."

"But what does that mean?"

"That certain places are not always good sources of food, but only at the right time."

The elephant covered his eyes with his trunk. He would have liked to bury himself in the ground. "But how can I, as governor, bring order to such chaos?" he whined in despair.

"I think the magic word is references. It is necessary to relate the information to each other to make it comparable."

"Yes!" trumpeted the elephant. "Then we can look at them both as a whole, or interpret them specifically for a place or time."

"Exactly!" The rhino was pleased to have found someone who understood. "And place and time are only the beginning. A dirty drinking fountain is a problem for many animals. I always get the runs from it. But the wild boars, they don't mind it at all. They drink it as if it were water from the noblest spring."

"You mean we also have to interpret differently depending on the animal?"

"Wouldn't that be wonderful to know both which sources have the highest overall quality, but to be able to recommend to each animal on its own whether it is suitable for drinking?"

"Yes, absolutely!"

"I'm just wondering where we should store all this information," the rhino mused with a frown that made his magnificent horn waver.

The elephant looked around searchingly. "We can't put it in the treetops anymore ..."

The rhino's gaze lingered on a long tree with a thick trunk full of brown bark. "What about the trunks?"

"Hm," the elephant thought. "That would be one possibility. We could put all the reference points there."

The rhino nodded enthusiastically. "I knew I'd come to the right place, my friend."

The elephant solemnly raised his trunk and let out a loud trumpet. "By the power of my office as governor of the jungle, I hereby appoint you my tribal adjutant! It will be your task to ensure the correct reference points and to ensure the harmony of our information. Are you ready to accept this new role?"

"The harmony of information." The rhinoceros nodded with emotion. "I gladly accept this role."

Practical application:
The rhino quickly understood that data harmonisation, the process of bringing data from different sources into a uniform format, is an important asset.

With the size of a company and the complexity of its business model, the heterogeneity of the data sources also grows. The higher the number of applications in the IT landscape, the greater the variety of connected data. And thus the heterogeneity of the data landscape.

The data of the different source systems are structured differently, and in the worst case even use different master data, which can be particularly pronounced in historically grown environments.

Having to bring this data together in a comparable form so that it can be compared and analysed is like a jigsaw puzzle with thousands of pieces that at first glance fit together well, but then nevertheless have subtle differences that make your life more difficult piece by piece.

Technologically, there are many ways to meet these challenges. Architectural concepts such as the data lake, the data warehouse or the data lakehouse are all suitable for dealing with the complexity. It depends on the situation, for example the type of data, the type of use cases and the way data is worked with in this context, which architecture suits you best. Concepts such as data virtualisation or data fabric can also be a powerful tool in companies with highly distributed, decentralised data to define harmonised data models while minimising the degree of data redundancy.

Much more important than the technical architecture is to address the crucial questions conceptually.

What data should be available in a harmonised form?

How can this data be structured so flexibly that it can be used for as many use cases as possible?

And in the end, as in this chapter, master data plays a crucial role. They are the link that makes aggregation, grouping, comparability and linking of data possible.

What master data is needed to flexibly aggregate and group the transaction data?

How is the master data maintained, mapped and kept up to date?

What roles and responsibilities are required for this in the governance model?

If you answer questions like these well, you will add great value to the reusability of your data, build trust in the harmonised data and be the rhino's best friend forever.

The Law of the Strongest

The elephant and the rhinoceros watched with amusement as the parrot frolicked with the dolphin. The colourful bird fluttered provocatively over the surface of the water and the dolphin tried to nudge him with his pointed nose.

"They are so carefree," the rhino remarked enviously.

"At the moment, yes," sighed the elephant. "But they also know that the humans are expanding. They have already cut down a seventh of the jungle. And we haven't found any ways to stop them yet. If they continue like this, we will soon have no habitat left."

"We have nevertheless significantly improved all our daily lives."

"Of course. But that's not enough."

"If we had the tiger on our side ..."

"Shoulda, coulda, woulda! That doesn't help us. He's so stubborn and in love with his own strength that he won't listen anyway."

"Nevertheless, we have done a lot," affirmed the rhino. "You are now governor, the harmony of information has been achieved and with the master data we have become much more flexible."

The elephant grumbled grumpily.

"Maybe we should call a conference of the animals again," the rhino mused. "Just listen to how things are going now with all these improvements ..."

The parrot settled busily on the tip of his nose: "Exactly! And we'll invite the tiger and the foolish hippo too!"

So three days later, the animals of the jungle met at the Sunny Glade in the heart of the jungle. There were many of them, a convinced community that exuberantly patted each other on the back for what they had already achieved.

"Never in my life have I been able to sleep so much," the sloth rejoiced. "Isn't it great? All this time, this restful quiet. Automation is the smartest invention in the world!"

The orangutan joined in the hymn of praise. "My head was buzzing from all the many things I could remember. I was able to distinguish thousands of plants just by their colour shades. Now I don't need that anymore. It has all become so simple."

"And I've never been less hungry than in the last few days," the bear grumbled contentedly. "So much food everywhere. Why didn't I see this before?"

Suddenly a murmur went through the crowd as the muscle-bound tiger made his way through the animals. His flaming eyes sparkled in the low sun. The magnificent fur shimmered. He bared his razor-sharp teeth menacingly and looked around condescendingly. The animals quickly lowered their heads to avoid looking him in the murderous eyes. The hippopotamus planted himself in the grass beside him, like a flabby bodyguard basking in the glory of his master.

"Quite an achievement you are reporting," the tiger growled maliciously. The hippo chuckled. "But we are also well-fed, as you can see. Strong and dangerous as ever. And we have no mumbo jumbo to blindly put our trust in. We drink where we have always drunk. We hunt where we have always hunted. And we think about the things we've always thought about. Does that make us feel bad?"

"But you could do even better," the parrot interjected defiantly.

"You have a few small successes to show, for all I care. But what was the target again that you were pursuing with the information?"

It should have been a rhetorical question, but the hippo immediately prepared to answer the tiger: "Stopping the humans!"

"And what have you achieved in this regard?"

The tiger's question cracked through the jungle like a whiplash. And no one answered him.

"That's what I thought," the tiger growled and made his way out of the crowd. The hippo followed at his heels and disappeared clumsily into the undergrowth with the sublime feline predator.

An oppressive silence fell over the clearing. The animals looked down at the ground, unable to look their companions in the eye. One could have heard a tumbling leaf fall to the mossy forest floor.

Then all at once the earth trembled.

"I've had enough of that old sourpuss!" the elephant thundered, stamping his mighty foot once more. "We're not going to let him get us down!"

At that moment the sun darkened as the mighty harpy eagle circled over the clearing with his dark grey wings. With a piercing cry, he swooped down and sat with sad black eyes in the circle of animals that stared at him as if spellbound.

"My eyes have seen terrible things," the bird of prey spoke in a clear voice, and the blood froze in the veins of the forest animals.

"What did you see?" whispered the parrot, whose wings were covered in goosebumps.

The eagle bowed his head. "My heart cannot put it into words." Then he pushed himself powerfully off the ground and spread his wings.

The animals followed his shadow until the harpy eagle had led them to the edge of the jungle. They pushed through the last foothills of the dense bushes, pushed thorny branches aside with their bodies and let their eyes wander over the endless expanse of the savannah.

The parrot let out a sharp cry. His otherwise dazzlingly colourful wings looked colourless as he plummeted to the ground, trembling. Thick tears ran down his beak.

The other animals also had tears in their eyes. Stunned, they stared at the countless carcasses of the steppe buffaloes lying bloodied in the dust, swarmed by flies.

The acrid stench of death crept inexorably into their noses. Whimpering, the parrot rammed his quivering beak into the earth. "Who is capable of such a thing?" he cried again and again until his voice broke.

The eagle spread a wing protectively over the parrot. "It was the humans. They hounded them. They killed them. They left them to rot in the scorching sun."

"For fun?" roared the parrot. "They killed them for fun?" The silence in the savannah was the only reply he received. "The tiger and the hippo are so right! How we have basked in our little successes. And how little we have achieved! Look what the humans have done! We are powerless to prevent it. It's all just useless gadgetry!"

Then the earth trembled again.

"It is cruel and distressing," thundered the elephant, stamping his mighty foot one more time. "But is that not the reason to continue our way undeterred? Yes, we could not prevent this bloodbath. And that makes me angry and sad too. But if we give up now, a tragedy like this will happen again and again!"

Slowly, the animals of the forest raised their heads. The thunder of the elephant had brought the fighting spirit back into their angry eyes.

"We've done so much already!" the jaguar roared. "Giving up is not an option!"

The snake hissed: "Probably we just haven't found the right approach to deal with the humans yet. But that doesn't mean it's impossible!"

"That's right," said the rhino in a calm voice. "Let us not despair, but carry on."

And on that day, in the blood-soaked savannah, the animals of the jungle made a vow not to rest until they had driven the humans out of their jungle.

Practical application:
On your way to becoming a data-driven company, there will also be resistance. Doubters who have not yet been convinced of the path you have chosen. Skeptics who are not very open to change. And grumblers who gloat over every small failure instead of learning and growing from failures.

Focus first on the 80 per cent who can be convinced. Use your energy to move forward side by side with these colleagues and also overcome setbacks with united forces.

The remaining 20 per cent will follow later, when the change has taken hold and the successes can no longer be denied.

As on any rocky journey, there can also be painful setbacks that give additional nourishment to the doubters. The elephant did not let these bitter failures deter him from his target.

What did you start your data-driven journey for? What can you learn from your failures? How can you turn even setbacks into positive energy and use it to facilitate further improvement?

The Self-service Animals

The cheetah took a short rest in a cosy clearing. The distance from the academy in the Dolphin´s Lagoon was long and led through impassable undergrowth. Everything was so strange, different from home in the endless steppe he longed to return to. The smells. The sounds. The impenetrable plant life.

But the steppe would never be the same again. Not after the bloodbath of the steppe buffaloes, which had shaken all the animals of the jungle to the core. After getting over the initial shock, he had rushed to the dolphin like many other animals. He wanted to learn everything he could about how to spin the information from the treetops. If only one of them had a bright idea on how to put an end to the disaster caused by humans.

His pointed ears heard a soft rustling. Quick as a flash, the cheetah lay in wait. All his senses were on alert. Something big and strong was making its way through the jungle. The cheetah's heart pounded. With a quick leap, he dashed forward and faced the jaguar, which flinched for a moment and then crouched on the ground, ready to pounce. The two cats eyed each other suspiciously. A rumbling growl came threateningly from their throats.

"Where are you going, jaguar?" asked the cheetah, still on guard.

"On the way to the lagoon."

"To the Dolphin´s Academy?"

"Yes, I want to do some more training to be able to support the governor in his work."

The cheetah relaxed a little. "That's where I come from."

"So, what did you think, cheetah?"

"Good," he replied curtly.

"That sounds like a but."

"No ... yes ... oh, I don't know."

"What's on your mind?"

"It all makes sense," the cheetah murmured with an uncertain shake of his head. "And yet ... I'm still missing something."

The jaguar frowned thoughtfully. "I know the feeling, my friend."

"Really?" the cheetah exclaimed in surprise. "Do you also feel frustrated that nature presents all the information prefabricated for you?"

The jaguar's eyes sparkled. *A soulmate at last!* "Yes, as magical as this whole thing is ... sometimes it really gets me down!"

"For example, when I want to eat, I find valuable information in the leaves. But some days I feel like ..."

"... for something very specific," the jaguar completed the sentence.

"There I have a ravenous appetite for ...", both animals exclaimed as if from the same mouth, bursting into snorting laughter.

The jaguar companionably placed a paw on his companion's shoulder and spoke: "There are days when I want to decide for myself who or what I eat."

"Exactly, and that's where the trees are not supposed to give me any suggestions that I don't feel like, but tell me where to find what I'm looking for."

The cheetah and the jaguar could hardly believe their luck. Finally, someone who understood them. Maybe they could find a way together.

"If there would be a way to tell the trees what you want ..." the cheetah mused.

"A way to limit the information that is displayed to you by deliberately using keywords ..."

Slowly, the cheetah stepped up to the bark of a tree. He followed an intuition, his feline instincts. It just felt right to put his paws on the bark. It was cool and rough, and he felt the life pulsating in the water veins of the ancient plant. As if of their own accord, the claws extended and dug into the bark, crunching. The predator performed an artfully curved movement and scratched two slightly curved horns into the bark of the tree.

As if by magic, the leaves in the treetops began to rustle. Astonished, the jaguar looked up. The images were changing. "A signpost," he breathed in disbelief.

The cheetah nodded and started to spurt. "Have you ever eaten gazelle?" he asked over his shoulder, laughing, and shot silently into the undergrowth.

"No, never," the jaguar replied, puzzled, and took up pursuit.

With a contented sigh, the jaguar and the cheetah feasted on the freshly killed gazelle.

"If we can communicate with nature through the bark," the cheetah smacked, "it opens up a whole new world of possibilities!"

"I can't imagine what you've managed to do."

"Yes, now I can eat what I want, when I want. And when I'm tired and don't want to run so fast, I just filter down to a slow prey that I can grab in slow running."

The jaguar licked his bloodstained paws clean with relish. "I don't dare say it," he whispered with a grin. "But I don't like the rain so much."

"A predator of the jungle is afraid of a few raindrops?" the cheetah was amused.

"If I tell you ... But now that we can exert so much influence all at once, surely it would be possible to combine the weather information with the hunting information, wouldn't it?"

"I suppose so," the cheetah nodded slowly.

The jaguar stepped to the next tree, scratched a complex image into the bark that resembled a sun and a crossed-out cloudburst. Then he drew a small rodent next to it and looked intently at his work.

Again there was a rustling in the treetops. And the jaguar received spot-on directions on how to go in search of rodents without getting wet.

"Incredible!" he marvelled hoarsely.

The two new friends looked at each other. Excitement flashed in their bright eyes. They knew they had discovered something big that would take the inhabitants of the jungle a giant step forward.

"Come with me!" the jaguar called excitedly.

"Where are you going?"

"To the Dolphin's Academy!"

"Oh, on your course," replied the cheetah. "That's where I just came from. I think it's time for me to return home."

"Forget my course!" the jaguar waved off, prancing restlessly from one paw to the other.

"Then what do you want so badly in the lagoon?"

"Well, what do you think! We have to tell the dolphin what we discovered."

"And then?"

"Then we ask him to add a new training course to his academy offerings and teach the other animals how to compile the information in the leaves on their own."

"Good idea!" cried the cheetah with twinkling eyes. "The animals will beat a path to the Dolphin´s Lagoon lagoon!" Then he became serious and looked wistfully at the sky. In his mind's eye he saw the cruelly mangled carcasses of the steppe buffaloes that still haunted his dreams at night. "This way, the animals of the forest will find ways to put a stop to the humans," he growled militantly.

"But what if they don't get along on their first attempts?" the jaguar mused.

"Then let them call us!" decided the cheetah, winking mischievously at the jaguar. "The two masters of the bark art will be happy to assist them in their first steps and give them valuable tips on how to bend the leaves to their will."

The two felines fell exuberantly into each other's arms and set off on velvet paws.

Practical application:

Limited resources are a major challenge in almost all companies. In the current labour market situation, it is not easy to find suitable professionals. And even if you keep increasing the central data and analytics team: the abundance of ideas and requirements will always catch up with you.

This makes it all the more important to specifically break down the dependence on a central data and analytics team. Empowering the business units to act independently and generate added value from their data circumvents the natural bottlenecks of centralised organisations. Agility and flexibility of the business units replace waiting for prioritisation by the data and analytics team.

Does this mean that the data and analytics team is no longer needed?

Quite the opposite! The role of the data and analytics team is more important than ever, but it has changed. Instead of implementing every requirement themselves, modern data and analytics teams should focus on providing high-quality self-service analytics tools and, based on this technological foundation, empower, support, guide and advise the business units. In addition to far-reaching training and consulting offers, you should provide a clear set of rules with processes and guidelines and work specifically towards establishing self-service analytics in the daily work processes.

It is important not to think exclusively of the reporting front ends. Of course, it is a valid first step to give the business the freedom to create reports and dashboards independently. Building on this, however, it is essential to work on giving the power users more flexibility in data preparation on the basis of the data warehouse or data lake.

As the transformation towards more responsibility for analytics in the business progresses, it makes sense to evaluate concepts such as the data mesh. The data mesh is a decentralised approach that shifts responsibility for data products to their functional business domains based on well-defined governance.

The Power of Community

"The cheetah and the jaguar were incredibly diligent," the dolphin lectured with twinkling eyes. "Here you will find a whole hundred leaves on which they wrote down examples of simple yet effective commands and neatly impaled them on a long branch."

The animals were amazed at this grandiose description of the high art of processing information for one's own purposes. With eyes wide open, they drooled at the branches piercing through countless colourful leaves.

"Don't worry," smiled the dolphin. "There's a branch for everyone. And the cheetah and the jaguar have asked me several times to mention that they'll be happy to support you once you take your first steps on your own."

Eager nodding of heads was the result. And none of the participants managed to take their eyes off the precious branches, as if they could disappear if one looked away for just a second.

With a flurry of joyful clicking sounds, the dolphin finished the training and threw one branch to each academy visitor with his deft snout.

With a lot of stomping, the animals streamed back into the jungle. Only a few of them stayed to talk to the exhausted dolphin for a moment.

"You did really well!" praised the elephant, tapping the dolphin's fin with his trunk. "Come on, let's have another fermented apple juice to celebrate the end of the day."

"Thank you. But this credit belongs to the cheetah and the jaguar alone. What an intuition! Unbelievable!"

"The jaguar and the cheetah ...", the rhino murmured. "I really would not have bargained on them at all."

"Me neither," the snake hissed. "But that was really a good training. So far, I have devoured every training course in no time. But today, it was like eating a full-grown cow. Excellent, I must say. Excellent!"

"I am curious to see what the animals will do with this knowledge," grumbled the elephant.

"Well, I have ambitious plans!" The snake ran his forked tongue over his fearsome fangs with relish. "I would like to sort my prey by size and then look at how easy it is to crawl in the respective terrain. I can already see myself slamming my fangs into their warm bodies."

The dolphin went over the violent vision in a gentle voice and steered the thoughts in another direction: "Wouldn't it be a great contribution to the community if we talked more about our ideas and use cases? I mean, everyone has their own idea of what is useful. And often you can spin the impulses of friendly animals further and adapt them for other purposes."

"Of course!" nodded the rhino. "That would certainly be useful."

"That would be valuable knowledge again, to be gobbled down like living meat!" the snake hissed.

The other animals rolled their eyes. But they liked the idea.

The elephant looked around. "Why don't we do it here with you, dolphin? Your lagoon is a beautiful place. And quiet as well. Just the right place for a regular exchange."

"And everyone already knows the way because of the academy," the rhino added.

The dolphin frowned. "Yes, the place would fit well." A brief hesitation. "But time worries me. The attendance keeps growing and the variety of trainings hardly leaves me time to juggle my balls. I'm not sure it's wise to take on too much."

Excited, the snake slithered between the massive legs of the rhino and the elephant. "What about me? Me, the snake?"

Suspiciously, the elephant looked at the snake.

"What is the matter with you? I will tell you why I am best suited for this task."

"Well, we're curious about that now."

"First of all, I'm bubbling over with ideas."

The rhino snorted softly. "With creepy bloody ideas, yes!"

"It doesn't matter. The other animals are welcome to reuse my ideas and adapt them to their less voracious requirements."

"Point taken!" the dolphin commented with a grin.

"And secondly?"

"Secondly, there is no one who devours information as much as I do. So I myself have the greatest interest in a good exchange. Doesn't that make me a suitable candidate?"

"Hm ... maybe ... But is there a third?"

"Thirdly, my eyes have a hypnotic effect. With just my gaze, I can get the animals to bluster out their knowledge. Isn't that what makes a good facilitator?"

Thoughtful silence.

"There is even a fourth," the snake triumphed. "They all respect my fangs. So if anyone can keep order here, it's me. Isn't that also an important qualification for a moderator?"

"All right, all right!" grumbled the elephant. "Let's just give it a try! But then we'll also have to use the regular meetings to tell the animals about the governor's latest rule book!"

"No problem. We can even discuss it and give you valuable feedback on how well the rule book works in the jungle undergrowth."

Satisfied, the elephant sat down on his broad butt and sipped his fermented apple juice. And the snake began to hiss excitedly in anticipation.

Practical application:

Do you want to change the data culture in your company for the long term? Then bring together enthusiastic and good power users to form a community. Show that you care about a living data culture by actively taking on leadership and moderation.

Through a community, you can promote a lively exchange on data and analytics topics. Users with an affinity for data are provided with a platform where they can present their own use cases and benefit from ideas from other business units.

There are different ways to set up such a community. It can be a pure experience exchange platform where power users share their achievements with each other. In addition, the representatives of the community can be used as multipliers to roll out governance aspects, guidelines or best practices in the business units, and to transparently communicate the service offerings of the central data and analytics team. In a very mature variant, it is even possible to actively involve the community in governance decisions, which is an excellent means of setting up practical governance and ensuring acceptance in the business units.

Which form best suits your company? How can a community make the greatest contribution to your company in terms of using tools and technologies more effectively, learning from each other and finding solutions to data-related problems together?

The Challenge of Diversity

And the animals exchanged ideas. Their ideas bubbled up as if there were no tomorrow. They outperformed each other in terms of creativity and usefulness.

"I've been keeping track of how much food of what kind there has been in what parts of the forest over the last few years," the bear grumbled proudly.

"Why are you so attached to the past?" the snake hissed. "Wouldn't it make more sense to retrieve this information on a daily basis?"

"For the small daily hunger," the bear answered and rubbed his belly, smacking his lips. "But I tell you: If you ever sleep for a whole winter, you will also have a bear's hunger. Then it can't be enough all at once." He grinned with plate-sized eyes at the illustrious round. "And the next time I choose a place to hibernate, I'll look for a cave that was teeming with food sources after winter the previous year. Then, even in a sleepy state, I can satisfy my bear's hunger."

The animals of the jungle nodded their heads appreciatively.
"Clever!"
"Anticipatory!"
"Survivalist!"

"Very nice example," the snake found. "Who would like to share another good use case with the other animals?"

The animals suddenly flinched as the chameleon emerged out of nowhere from the shade of a dark green plant. Uncertainly, he looked around and cleared his throat.

"You know I shy away from the big stage," he began in a low voice. "But since all your cases are about eating, I want to show you that the information can be used in other ways."

"Not to eat?" the bear marvelled.

"No, I use it to NOT get eaten," smiled the chameleon, earning interested looks. "When I set out to roam the jungle, I do a colour analysis of the possible paths to my destination."

"And what good is that? Just take the shortest way," yawned the sloth.

"It is not the length of the journey that determines a safe and peaceful arrival."

"But?"

"If I want to arrive safely, I have to be able to camouflage myself well everywhere along the way. Otherwise, I'm far too easy a prey."

The snake hissed appreciatively. "So the purpose of the colour analysis is to make sure you can imitate all the colours in your path."

"Correct," nodded the chameleon. "The treetops even calculate the deviations for me."

"And then you choose the shortest route where you can camouflage yourself sufficiently?"

"No."

Questioning looks pierced the chameleon. "But why not?"

"Oh, friends, you don't know how exhausting it is to change colours all the time. And some shades cost me more energy than others."

"So you're looking for the safest route with the least effort?" the sloth marvelled, eyes twinkling.

The chameleon nodded and retreated back into the shadows.

"What a great contribution," praised the snake. "Would any other animal like to step forward and use this stage?"

The cormorant swung down from the branch of a tree and settled proudly and loftily in the middle of the animal circle. "Yes, I have another use case where I kill two birds with one stone."

"You killed other birds? I thought you cormorants ate fish."

"Exactly, that's the point. You all use the information about our waters, right?"

The animals nodded in agreement. "Sure, to drink only the best and healthiest water the jungle has to offer."

"That's how I do it as well," said the cormorant. "Only that I add the information of whether there are tasty fish in there."

"That's great when you can eat and drink in the same place!"

"Exactly. It saves me a lot of time!"

"Really great what you are all doing with the information," purred the snake. "Now we come to the key question of today." The animals stared expectantly at their host. "Has anyone found a way to contain the danger from the humans yet?"

Silence fell over the clearing. They all looked down at the ground.

"I follow their spread every day," said the jaguar. "And if necessary, I adjust my territory accordingly to avoid them."

"Yes, me too!" many other inhabitants of the jungle confirmed as if from the same mouth.

"So we found a way to avoid them," the snake summed up with sad eyes. "But not how to stop them from spreading. So we continue to delay the inevitable."

The devastating truth lingered in the air. The images of the cruelly mauled steppe buffalos still haunted their minds. No one wanted to end up like that.

"We have so much information at our disposal. Why haven't any of us found a way to use it to fight the humans?"

At first, the animals were silent. They looked thoughtfully into the trees, as if they could expect a helpful answer from there. But none came.

"It's so much information," the bear stammered. "It's hard enough for me to keep track of what I need to secure my beloved meals with."

"Yes, exactly!" the cheetah also exclaimed. "I only know really well what I use every day. It's just too much!"

"I, too, have slowly but surely lost track," confirmed the parrot.

The snake nodded thoughtfully. "Yes, I know that feeling. Overwhelmed by such a flood of information that even I can't gulp down in one bite. Maybe we have all the information we need to successfully fight the humans and we just don't see it yet."

"If we had a better overview," the cheetah reflected, "it would be easier and faster to use the information even more profitably."

The jaguar took the thought further. "We would need some kind of list of what information the jungle has to offer in the first place!"

"Like a catalogue!" cried the cheetah.

The snake was beside himself with joy. "Yes, that sounds good. And if you have an overview of all the information, then you can specifically access the information you need for your use case!"

The animals of the jungle cheered. It was a groundbreaking idea.

"Who is the fastest of you?" asked the snake.

"Me, of course!" the cheetah hissed.

"Then run quickly to the elephant and ask him if he, in his role as governor, can initiate the creation of such a catalogue!"

And the cheetah dashed away.

Practical application:
A successful transformation to a data-driven company brings new challenges.

The lower the data usage in the company, the easier it is for a central data and analytics team (as well as the few power users) to keep track of all data sources.

Increased diversity in use cases and user groups, as well as the increasing dynamics and complexity of use cases, are very positive signs of increased data use and thus a tangible indication of the rapid development of a data culture.

However, this development places completely new demands on the transparency and documentation of data.

The democratisation of data and easy access to the data needed are among the most important success factors of the data-driven company. And a well-documented, ideally highly automated data catalogue is a significant prerequisite for this.

A data catalogue is a repository in which descriptive information about the available data is catalogued, for example definitions, origin, relationships or other useful metadata.

A well-founded data catalogue should separate technical documentation from the documentation of business meaning ("business glossary") and above all make the data stewards in the business units responsible for creating and maintaining the business glossary.

The core objective of the data catalogue is transparency. Transparency as to which data is available in which form, from which sources the data originates, who the responsible contact persons are and how one can get access to this data.

Even though the lack of documentation is one of the most common challenges in data use, the effort required for comprehensive documentation is often very high. An important success factor is therefore once again automation. The better the capabilities of your data platform to automatically extract and contextualise metadata, the more efficiently you can use your data landscape.

Nevertheless, the professional use of leading data catalogue or data intelligence platforms requires a fundamental maturity in data governance and data culture.

Is your company ready to take full advantage of the added value of this significant investment? Or would it be a better first step to start with a small solution and grow as maturity progresses?

Summary Part 2

The animals of the jungle quickly realised that automation and the definition of visualisation standards are not enough. The development of a data culture needs a much broader foundation.

With the establishment of the Data Academy, all animals were given free access to more data literacy.

A data governance model provides a target-oriented set of rules as a breeding ground for joint work with information.

Intensive communication measures and the harmonisation of data and master data paved the way for the animals to obtain information from data flexibly and independently by introducing self-service analytics.

The animals do not let bitter setbacks deter them from their path, but learn from their experiences together in a community.

By introducing a data catalogue, they finally laid another foundation stone. The improved access to well-documented data continues to drive the data culture.

Part 3

... in which the animals of the forest take the final step towards a data-driven jungle on the basis of the foundation that has been created.

The Magic of Lighthouses

Under the leadership of the elephant, the animals of the jungle established a catalogue that was something to behold. All the animals were allowed to make their contribution and enter and describe the information they used in it.

And once again, this opened up completely new possibilities. They now had a great overview of what information was available to them. And the exchange moderated by the snake was bubbling over with ideas.

But there was no effective idea of how to drive the humans out of the forest.

"We're not getting anywhere, no matter what we do," the rhino whined dejectedly.

The snake was also frustrated. "I had imagined it all to be easier."

"We would have to stick together even more."

"But we do!"

"Not all of them!"

"You mean the tiger and the hippo?"

"Especially the tiger," murmured the rhinoceros. "He is quite simply the strongest, the most lethal of us!"

"Yes, you are probably right. Without his support, it will be hard to survive."

The rhinoceros thought for a long time. "Maybe the dolphin knows some advice?"

"Let's try," the snake hissed, and they set off.

"What can I do for you, my friends?" the dolphin greeted the visitors in a friendly manner.

"It's the tiger," the rhino explained. "We must finally find a way to include him or we are doomed."

The dolphin gazed thoughtfully out to sea, which stretched endlessly beyond the lagoon to the horizon. The waves swayed in the gentle wind. The distant roar had a calming and inspiring effect.

Patiently, the rhino and the snake watched the clever mammal.

"Out at sea, humans have built lighthouses," the dolphin finally said. The two visitors listened spellbound. "They are tall towers that rise up into the sky on islands or cliffs. They shine and glow to guide the way."

The dolphin paused for a moment, letting his words sink in, before continuing his thought. "We need something like that for the tiger too. A dazzling lighthouse, a use case that will convince him enough to join us."

The rhino shook his head sadly. "As far as that is concerned, we have already tried everything. Ask the parrot. He literally talked his head off."

The snake agreed. "But the tiger is just as stubborn as the old hippo!"

"It is not just about the tiger, but also about us," the dolphin suggested in a gentle voice.

"About us? But we're doing everything right!"

"Nobody does everything right. We probably do a lot of things well. Still, we haven't found a way to convince the tiger."

"And that's despite him knowing all our great use cases!"

The dolphin smiled. "But perhaps mere use cases are not enough for him."

"What do you mean?"

"We always explain to him how we are using the information and what we are trying to achieve."

"But what else should we explain to him?"

"The impact this is having!" cried the dolphin.

"Impact?"

"Yes, measurable and tangible results. Facts and figures instead of use cases!"

"A measurable impact," the rhino murmured thoughtfully.

"Facts and figures," repeated the snake with huge eyes.

The dolphin gave them an encouraging nod. "Maybe it's time to convene the next regular exchange."

"Yes," replied the snake. "It's time."

And so the snake explained to the community of animals what the dolphin had advised them. "We need your most shining examples so that we can bring them to the attention of the tiger and the hippo. And not just your use cases. No, that alone won't do. What we need are measurable results, tangible added values, facts and figures!"

The bear trudged with heavy steps into the middle of the circle.

"I'm feeling better than ever since I started foraging with the forest's information," he grumbled. "I feel stronger, fitter and am no longer so grumpy and sleepy."

"All well and good, but can you back that up in figures?" the snake inquired.

"I've gained a massive 24 pounds since then. 24 pounds!" the bear growled, his eyes twinkling. "Unfortunately, I don't have the intelligence to convert that into a percentage."

"That should be about four per cent," marvelled the dolphin.

The bear grinned up to both ears. "Wow, four per cent for sure is a lot!"

"And how did you do that?"

"My stomach has been growling all day. That's the way it is when you're a bear. And often my stomach tells me what to stuff into me next to get ready for hibernation."

"And then?"

"When I had my bear's hunger, I listened to my gut and stuffed it in."

"But then how could you gain another four per cent?"

"Quite simply, I no longer trust my gut feeling. It only tells me what I'm craving at the moment. But not what is most nutritious for my winter fat. Now I eat what serves its purpose and prepares me for hibernation in the best possible way, and not what my stomach is rumbling for at the moment."

"Excellent," the snake hissed delightedly. "Four per cent more fighting weight through carefully chosen foraging. That should please the tiger!"

The jaguar replaced the bear in the middle of the circle. He looked proud and strong into the circle before he started to tell about his achievements.

"My territory has always been quite small for a jaguar," he said. "For a long time, deep in my heart, I have longed to increase that territory."

"Why have you never dared before?" asked the snake.

"Because I thought it was risky. I didn't want to risk a fight to the death with another jaguar. Or even with the tiger."

"And how is it today?"

"Today I have expanded my territory by a whole ten per cent," the jaguar replied proudly.

"Ten per cent?" the cheetah marvelled. "That's awesome, my friend! How did you manage that?"

"I used the information to study which animals roam along the borders of my territory at regular intervals. So I studied where exactly the territories of other predatory cats border my territory."

"And then you expanded your territory in places where you were not in danger," the cheetah concluded, impressed.

The jaguar nodded.

"Excellent example," hissed the snake. "And measurable at that. Ten per cent enlargement of the territory by studying the roaming behaviour of neighbouring animals. Great! That should be of burning interest to a territorial fanatic like the tiger."

At the end of the exchange, the parrot fluttered into the centre of the round. As the undisputed evangelist of the animals' innovations, he was highly respected among all the participants. Silence descended over the lagoon.

"Three days ago I did an exciting evaluation with the filtering mechanisms that the cheetah and the jaguar discovered for us." He took a deep breath. A thoroughly skilful dramatic pause. "I wanted to know how the deaths among the animals of the jungle have developed since we began our project."

With eyes wide with interest, the animals stared at the parrot as if transfixed.

"Well?" the snake whispered into the tense silence.

"Before the start of our project, births and deaths balanced each other out - plus/minus one per cent. So the number of animals in the jungle has been relatively constant for years."

"And how is it today?"

"Similar - there were just under one per cent more births than deaths."

Disappointed, the animals let the air escape from their lungs. They had expected an imposing announcement, an irrefutable evaluation. What a disappointment!

"That's it?"

"So none of this has made any difference?"

"Not quite," warbled the parrot in a loud voice. The disappointed heads jerked upwards. Their gazes were glued to his beak. "You have to look at these numbers in context."

"The parrot speaks in riddles," grumbled the bear, scratching his head in confusion.

"Actually, it's quite simple," replied the parrot. "In the areas where humans have spread, there have been forty per cent more deaths than births."

A shadow flitted across the faces of the animals. A terrible number. A harbinger of what lay ahead for them.

"But in all other areas, since we have been working specifically with information, we have ten per cent more births than deaths."

The animals nodded silently. This was truly good news.

The snake's throat-clearing ended the thoughtful silence. "So it's safe to say that using information in areas without new external influences increases the conservation of our species by ten per cent?"

"Yes, you can," affirmed the parrot.

After the session, which ended with frenetic applause, the snake, the rhinoceros and the parrot were left alone in the clearing.

"A good result, don't you think?" the snake summed up.

"Yes, absolutely! If the tiger can't be convinced this way, then we don't stand a chance," agreed the rhino.

"We just need to work on how to sell the information to the tiger," sighed the parrot.

"You are our evangelist," said the snake.

"Yes," nodded the rhino. "If anyone can find a way, it's you!"

And the parrot withdrew to practise his speech for the tiger.

Practical application:

If you want to convince the last doubters of your path on your data-driven journey, this is rarely successful via creative ideas and ambitious goals alone.

Doubters do not want to see dreamy visions, but can usually only be swayed by tangible evidence.

Use your successful initiatives to do this and back up each use case with a clear business case. This means you need concrete numbers that demonstrate measurable success. And you should focus on what you have already achieved. Because no one can doubt results that can be proven in facts and figures - but ambitious goals and optimistically calculated promises can be doubted.

Communication plays a major role in such lighthouses. Sell your initiatives, publicise achieved goals and thus spread the high added value of data in your company.

Using concrete examples such as the "hibernation use case" of the hungry bear, shows that sound and demonstrable information leads to better (because data-driven) decisions than simply listening to one's gut feeling.

You should tell a story in your communication measures ("storytelling") in order to present the initiative and its results in a tangible, understandable and interesting way.

Link the communication to your data literacy offerings so that stakeholders who want to jump on the bandwagon based on the results have a first point of contact.

And here too, use the community as a multiplier to spread your shining examples to all departments and business units.

Which first lighthouse will you use to convince your stakeholders of the benefits of data-driven initiatives?

The Pains of the Tiger

Fearlessly, the tiger roamed through the thicket. He knew that he was blending perfectly into his jungle. Invisibly and silently, he worked his way through the undergrowth.

This information mania of the other animals is sheer nonsense, he thought. *But the humans make me nervous too. What do they want here? Why are they clearing such large parts of our primeval forest?*

On velvet paws, he crept on. Muscles as supple as the wind. Strong, fast and deadly.

Two more miles, then I can probably already observe the humans up close.

Suddenly the tiger stopped. Thunderstruck, he stared through a small opening in the dense undergrowth. With a pounding heart, he took another step closer. And opened his eyes in disbelief.

That fast? They shouldn't be here yet! His thoughts raced. *How can humans spread so far in such a short time?*

The tiger ducked deep into the undergrowth and slowly pushed forward. He had to get to the bottom of this. The bushes gave his massive striped body perfect cover.

But the tiger did not know that a human scout was sitting high up in a tree, attentively scanning the surroundings with binoculars.

The warning call came completely unexpectedly. "Watch out, a tiger!" The king of the jungle was shaken to the core.

Cursing, the tiger retreated. But the bushes were thick and impassable. He heard excited shouts. And footsteps. Many footsteps.

Then a deafening bang thundered in his head. The tiger growled. A piercing beep settled on his tortured ears. And again there was a bang. Even louder. Even more terrifying.

Snarling, he sprinted through the undergrowth. Branches and bushes tore his fur. But he didn't care. He just wanted to get away, away from this ominous thunder.

The next bang. A yelp escaped his throat. Hot and burning, something bit into his left flank and made him stumble. The sudden pain made the mighty cat stagger.

The voices grew louder. And the footsteps came closer.

The tiger struggled through the thicket with a limp. The wound burned like fire. But his pursuers gave him no respite. He collapsed. He struggled to his feet again. He limped on, his face contorted in pain. Until the voices became quieter and the footsteps stopped.

Exhausted, he let himself fall into the bushes. His body shook. Breathing heavily, he clenched his teeth to keep from shouting out loud. He had underestimated the humans. A fatal mistake.

What if they keep chasing me? What if more of them come and pick up my scent? What if this thing that bit me poisons my body? Fear constricted his throat.

Then he heard a familiar voice in the distance. Slowly he crept closer. His legs trembled with exertion. But he was quite sure. These were not humans. It was the parrot.

The parrot sat alone on a tree stump, gesticulating wildly and giving a fiery speech. The tiger strained to squint his eyes, but he could see no audience.

"A tiger is strong! Stronger than all of us!" the parrot fluted to his fictional listeners and raised his right wing in the air in an admonishing manner. "And yet four per cent fighting weight and a territorial expansion of ten per cent cannot harm a tiger either. On the contrary! What advantages that could have. The information is there, literally waiting to be used profitably. And ten per cent more births than deaths cannot be dismissed. Listen to your heart, and let these shining examples guide you!"

The words echoed through the forest and fell silent. Then the parrot hopped off the tree stump and hung his head and both wings powerlessly.

"I can practise, practise and practise again," sighed the parrot resignedly. "In the end, we won't convince the tiger after all. And then it was all for nothing."

Then the tiger crawled out of his hiding place, breathing heavily, and looked at the parrot with a mixture of pity and melancholy.

The motley bird stared at the otherwise majestic feline predator. The tiger was only a shadow of his former self. Breathing heavily, he lay powerless on the ground in front of him, shaking like a leaf. Then the parrot's eyes swept over the flank and saw the many drops of blood oozing from the wound.

"Maybe you don't have to convince me anymore," the tiger whispered wearily. "The humans have already proved me wrong."

Then he collapsed and his world went black.

Practical application:
You can reach a lot going bottom-up. But you can only become a truly data-driven company if you take your management level with you top-down and convince them of the benefits. The animals of the jungle have recognised this, and the parrot has once again put a lot of effort into this communication.

The tiger had to learn the hard way and came to the late and traumatic realisation that he had probably taken the wrong path.

It does not have to be so dramatic that the colleagues who ignore data at the beginning fail fundamentally. Try to prevent this and bring these doubters (especially those from the management level) along with you beforehand by means of concrete added values, tangible results and measurable outcomes. Make sure that you don't end up like the parrot, which unfortunately was simply too late in this chapter.

A New World

Hastily, the parrot fluttered through the bushes. Branches whipped on his wings. Thorns bored into the proud colourful plumage. But the panting parrot ignored the pain. Bravely, he dashed ahead, searching the undergrowth as if out of his mind. There was only one animal who could help. And he was anything but easy to find.

Then the parrot caught sight of a shy movement. Something large was slowly retreating into the thicket.

"No, don't leave!" the parrot cried, desperation speaking from his broken voice. The tiger was not loved in the jungle. But he was heard, feared and respected. What would their jungle be without the tiger's mighty paws? And what future did they have if he was lost forever? "Wait, we need your help!"

"My help?" whispered a timid voice.

"Yes, your healing powers."

Cautiously, a small, narrow, pointed head peeked out from behind a tree trunk. "My healing powers?"

"That's right."

With a furrowed brow, the giant pangolin bent over the unconscious tiger, whom the elephant and the rhinoceros had carried through the jungle with their combined strength on a makeshift stretcher made of branches and bushes.

"Something is stuck in his flank," the giant pangolin murmured thoughtfully. "It's barely leaking blood, but the tiger has lost a lot of lifeblood."

"How can we help him?" the parrot asked impatiently.

The giant pangolin felt the forehead of the massive feline predator. "Hot! Way too hot."

"Shall we fetch water?" offered the chalky elephant.

"Cooling compresses of damp leaves?" the rhino called out in a trembling voice.

The fate of the tiger was very close to all of them. He, of all animals, had always been so strong and invincible.

"We must fight the cause of the evil," said the giant pangolin. "The wound has become infected."

He detached a scale from his massive body and ground it into a fine brown powder with a stone. The parrot, the elephant and the rhinoceros watched every little movement with interest.

"We have to hope we can stop the inflammation," whispered the giant pangolin, carefully blowing the dust of his scale directly onto the wound.

"Now it's a matter of waiting."

The parrot fluttered excitedly from branch to branch. The elephant stepped restlessly from one leg to the other. And the rhinoceros rubbed his pointed horn against an old tree without stopping.

Suddenly the cheetah and the jaguar burst through the bushes, panting. "We tried everything!"

"Well?" the parrot inquired expectantly. "Did you find anything?"

"We searched the catalogue, consulted the trees, even asked the wise dolphin for advice ..."

"Don't keep us in suspense!" the elephant rumbled indignantly. "Speak up!"

"Nothing," confessed the cheetah and the jaguar. "We haven't found anything at all."

"But there must be something to it."

"No. Nothing. Nothing at all," the cheetah repeated.

"Obviously, there is no empirical data on this case," added the jaguar.

Then the tiger stirred. With his face contorted in pain, he looked from one animal to the other.

"How am I doing?" His voice was no more than a hoarse whisper.

The giant pangolin felt the tiger's forehead and lowered his eyes dejectedly. "The fever has risen."

The predatory cat's wistful eyes took hold of the parrot, which tried valiantly to swallow his tears.

"For once I dared to bite the bullet," whispered the tiger. "And then I let myself be struck down by such stupid human devilry."

"You couldn't have known that they could strike you down with their magic from afar," sniffed the parrot, compassionately placing his wing on the wounded tiger's belly, which rose and fell in laboured breaths.

The tiger's clenched fangs twisted into a sarcastic grin. "Yes. If I had known, I would certainly have taken cover."

Then the blackness enveloped him again.

"But there must be something we can do!" cried the parrot desperately.

The other animals shook their heads in silence and looked down at the ground.

"I'm not giving up that easily!" cried the parrot, trembling. "Not in my back yard!"

And then he flew away until the distant treetops swallowed him up.

"Poor parrot," murmured the elephant. "Of all of us, he carried the greatest hope in his heart."

Sobbing, the parrot crouched on a branch. Thick tears dripped from his colourful plumage. When he opened his eyes again, two hummingbirds were sitting to his right and left, looking at him pityingly.

"Why are you so sad?" they asked in bright, clear voices that sounded like bells.

"It's the tiger ..." the parrot sniffed. "He is dying. And there's nothing we can do for him."

"Why not?"

"There is no information in the whole jungle on how to cure him."

"But our primeval forest is not the only forest in the world."

With wide eyes, the parrot looked up and stared at the tiny hummingbird. "Not the only forest?" he stammered, stunned.

"Of course not. We have seen many forests on our travels."

"Many forests ...", the parrot mused. Then his countenance suddenly brightened. "You are geniuses!"

The flock of hummingbirds was enormous. With nimble wing beats, they hovered silently in the air and listened to the parrot's instructions.

"It's a matter of survival for all of us! Swarm out, brave hummingbirds, to save our king of the jungle! Fly out and find other forests in faraway lands. And return soon to bring us information on how to cure the tiger."

Excitedly, the hummingbirds fluttered up and down.

"Take these branches with you on your journey. They come from the clearing where the unicorn's magic horn touched the ground and brought the information to life. Perhaps you can store the information from distant forests in these branches."

And the flock of hummingbirds took off. Their tiny wings carried them off in all directions. And the parrot stared after them enviously.

"Fly fast, my little friends. For time is running out …"

Practical application:
In this chapter, the animals take another step on their data-driven journey: For the first time, they go beyond the internal data of their jungle and begin to tap into external data sources.

External data sources are becoming increasingly crucial to provide a comprehensive basis for decision-making in fast-moving, dynamic business fields.

Supplement your internal data in a meaningful way and look specifically for the missing pieces of the puzzle to create a complete database that you need for your business. Find out about suitable marketplaces for data and check data service providers in your industry.

Think as broadly as possible about what kind of external data adds the most value to your business. Is it important in your environment to analyse data from social media? Does weather data play a role in your business field? Do you have all the necessary market information such as market shares or complete and up-to-date product master data?

Be creative, but always keep an eye on costs and benefits, as buying external data also incurs costs. Ensure that your data investments are reusable by coordinating well within your organisation what external data has already been tapped and how it can be used. Among other things, the data catalogue also plays a decisive role here.

The Oracle

And the little hummingbirds flew. They flew fast, they flew far, and they all brought branches bursting with information from other forests.

Hastily, the parrot rushed to the giant pangolin and announced the good news.

"How is he?" he inquired with a worried look at the sleeping tiger, whose chest was barely rising and falling with the tortured breaths.

"It doesn't look good," whispered the giant pangolin. "He hasn't been awake for hours and he's very, very weak."

"Come with me for a moment," the parrot asked and led the giant pangolin to a mighty tree trunk. Around the tree, countless small branches were stuck in the ground. Curious, the giant pangolin looked around. "Now we will see if we can still save the tiger."

As if on cue, the jaguar and the cheetah burst out of the undergrowth and set to work. With nimble paws, they carved an animal body and a human with a long stick into the bark of the tree. There was a soft rustling in the treetops. Concentrated, the giant pangolin watched every movement of the leaves. Sweat beaded from his forehead. Then the healer of the forest nodded thoughtfully.

"Does that help you?" urged the parrot.

The giant pangolin wrinkled his scales. "Possibly," he said mysteriously.

"Do you know what we have to do?"

"Yes. The thing is called a bullet, which is stuck in the tiger's body and poisons him from the inside. We must remove this bullet. Only then will the powder of my ground scales take their full effect." There was a brief pause. "If we are not too late."

"Then let's get going!" the cheetah shouted excitedly.

And so, following the guidance of the treetops, the giant pangolin performed the first surgery in the history of the jungle.

The tiger was weak, bedded at death's door with rattling breath. But the bullet had been removed.

The jaguar eyed the tiger as he writhed, twitching, in uncontrolled spasms of fever. "Did it work?"

"I did everything according to plan," groaned the giant pangolin, exhausted. "Now all we can do is wait."

Two days later, the parrot was sitting at the tiger's bedside. The mighty predator already looked much stronger. The movements seemed more supple. The fever had disappeared. And he had an appetite for raw meat again.

"How are you today?"

"Much better," the tiger confirmed with relief. "You have saved my life, my friends."

The parrot eyed the striped mountain of muscle. "You look very thoughtful," he said with a serious expression.

"Do you remember our conversation when the fever knocked my lights out?" asked the tiger.

"You're asking me? You were the one with the delirium," the parrot teased.

"Maybe I am sometimes wiser in this state than when I am well."

"What do you mean?"

"If I had known they were going to shoot at me, I would certainly have taken cover."

"Yes, that would have been sensible."

The tiger nodded. "You have already achieved a lot. But you are always running after the information. You are looking back, trying to understand what is."

"Yes, we do. And so much has improved as a result."

"But wouldn't it be even better to know what will be?"

The parrot's breath caught. "We are supposed to … look into the future?"

The tiger smiled. "We should use the information to paint a probable picture of the future, yes."

Stunned, the parrot stared at the tiger. His thoughts were racing. The hoarse voice of the colourful bird was no more than an awed whisper: "You ... are a genius!"

The deep growl of the big cat was almost gentle for a deadly predator of his size. "I am only carrying on the thoughts you have so boldly brought into the world."

The jungle was in turmoil. Leaves rustled. Branches cracked. Animals roamed through the undergrowth. And at the Sunny Glade, they all came together to revolutionise their joint information project.

Strong and sublime, the tiger stepped into the middle of the huge circle. He was still limping slightly, but that did not detract from his majestic aura. His fiery gaze swept over the animals of the forest. And they were filled with pride and gratitude. His powerful voice echoed through the clearing.

"You have started an impressive journey, dear friends. And even though I was sceptical at the beginning, your great ideas saved my life in the end. And for that, I thank you all!" As if spellbound, the inhabitants of the jungle hung on his lips. "Now it is time for us to take the next step. Let's develop your vision and drive the humans out of our lands once and for all!"

Cheers roared across the clearing like thunder. The tiger bared his fearsome fangs eager to fight.

"It is good that we know the past. But no one can change what was. It is the future for which we must sharpen our gaze."

"But how should we look into the future?"

The cheetah stepped up to the tiger's side. "There are patterns in the information, recurring developments."

"That's right," cried the tiger. His eyes flashed. "It's good to know where the best food is at the moment. But it's even better to set up your territory where the best food will be in the future!"

The animals nodded excitedly. The bear licked his lips.

"And it is good to know where humans are currently spreading out. But it is even more important that we understand what they plan to do next. Then we can take precautions, set traps. And we may be able to foil their plans!"

Deafening cheers filled the clearing in the heart of the jungle. The animals knew they had a chance with the tiger's full support.

"I see the hope and confidence sparkling in your eyes," the tiger spoke, his voice taking on a cautionary undertone. "But humans are powerful and dangerous! I have experienced it myself. If we want to avert the impending disaster, then we must focus on the most important issue: On how we can stop the humans."

The animals listened intently.

"No more gimmicks, no more unnecessary sideshows. Humans are now our full priority!"

"But we have to eat too!" protested the bear.

"Yes, we have to. But when humans have cut down the entire jungle, we will starve in any case!"

The gloomy prospects echoed menacingly from the trees.

"All our thoughts must now turn to developing forecast models and testing their accuracy. From now on, we will meet here in the Sunny Glade every third day. And everyone brings their models, test results and information. On this basis, we will jointly make decisions on how to stop the humans!"

And the animals of the forest obeyed and set to work.

Practical application:
In this fundamental chapter, the animals of the jungle have made two groundbreaking improvements. Firstly, they continue to develop their project in the direction of advanced analytics. And secondly, they experience true data-driven leadership from the tiger for the first time.

Many interesting use cases can be covered by backward-looking reporting. Looking into the past, understanding correlations and analysing developments are valuable sources for making good decisions.

But being able to predict the future is an even more powerful tool that you should definitely not disregard. Use the existing data from your reporting system and analyse how you can develop high-quality predictive models based on the data patterns.

Are there already Data Scientists in your data and analytics team who have specialised in this combination of mathematical and statistical knowledge, IT know-how and business understanding?

This allows you to stay ahead of the competition by, for example, improving decision-making processes with more reliable forecasts or optimising your marketing and sales strategies by predicting customer behaviour.

The tiger, in his majestic leadership, has linked this step with a very important development: he has demonstrated true data-driven leadership and established a data-driven meeting culture.

Do you have clear rules in your meetings that decisions should be made based on data, predictive models and facts?

The most important success factor here is that the manager himself must exemplify this culture by not acting as a "hippo" (highest paid person's opinion) in decision-making and by not making the decisions he believes to be right - ignoring data and facts - based on his organisational position of power.

Only when leaders make decisions based on the facts at hand, regardless of their position, can they establish a truly data-driven meeting culture characterised by transparency and open discourse based on data and facts.

And if the data-driven energy is then directed towards a concrete goal, as the tiger does with his clear prioritisation, in order to impose the right focus on the sometimes somewhat digressive animals that are self-absorbed in their data-driven sideshows, then nothing more stands in the way of a data-driven leadership culture.

But there is another important lesson from this chapter: never close the door!

The animals of the forest could have punished the tiger with ignorance for his previous behaviour. But instead, they welcomed the reformed tiger with open arms.

You too are bound to encounter sceptics on your data-driven journey. Because everyone deals with change and new ideas in a different way. With your data-driven success stories, you can inspire some late bloomers to follow your path. Always keep the door open and welcome all colleagues who want to jump on the bandwagon!

Summary Part 3

The animals of the forest had already laid a strong foundation for a data-driven jungle, but the use of the information was not yet mature enough to speak of a fully comprehensive data culture.

But through targeted lighthouse projects, they were able to convince even the last doubters and, through a twist of fate with the tiger, integrate their most important leadership figure.

By tapping into external data sources and introducing predictive analytics, animals are taking the final steps towards a data-driven jungle in which leadership and decision-making culture are also based on data, information and facts and no longer on the law of hierarchy and strength.

Part 4

... in which the animals of the forest professionalise their handling of data and expand their toolbox of methods.

The Dark Side of Power

Yawning, the sloth settled down on the green shore of the small lake and enjoyed the last rays of the evening sun, which slowly disappeared behind the distant treetops. It was a picturesque sight, and the sloth loved to doze in peace and solitude. Deeply he sucked the earthy scent of the damp ground into his nose and sighed comfortably.

Then the sloth heard small, clumsy footsteps. With a roll of his eyes, he turned onto his belly and peered towards the shore. He stared intently at the spot where he had suspected the sound. But there was nothing to be seen. Or was there?

An inconspicuous movement caught his attention. Like an invisible shadow that crept along the shore to feast on the tasty fresh water of the lake.

"I should have guessed," the sloth finally laughed. "The chameleon!"

Caught off guard, the scaly iguana raised his head and stared at the sloth. "Oh, it's you!" The chameleon pushed the air out of his lungs in relief.

"Why the caution?"

"What do you mean?"

"Well, it's not normal for you to be so elaborately camouflaged while drinking by the lakeside that you'd think you'd seen a ghost."

"Oh ... well ...", the reptile pressed around.

"What's the matter?"

"I ... well ... I'm scared!"

"Scared?" The sloth rolled his eyes skeptically. "But of what? We live in the age of jungle information. The leaves tell you where you can eat and drink without worry. And where I can sleep peacefully and undisturbed. Now we can also make predictions. And soon we will even expel the humans. What else should we animals be afraid of?"

The chameleon glanced nervously left and right. Then he crept closer to the sloth and whispered conspiratorially: "Have you never asked yourself who benefits from all this? Haven't you ever wondered who gets what benefit from it?"

"No, I'm happy and content right now and I've never been able to lie so lazily and relaxed in the evening sun before."

"That's just like you," whispered the chameleon reproachfully. "Naive and thoughtless as ever."

"Yes, but why not? Life is far too beautiful to spend all day grumbling about it!"

But the reptile was not deterred. "Just look at this bank here. The forest knows exactly that there is pure and healthy drinking water here. And doesn't it also know who comes and goes here, who drinks here and when? Can't you ask all our behaviour patterns from the trees?"

"Of course you can. But that's the magic of this new world. The magic that allowed us to simplify our lives."

"But what if someone has ulterior motives?"

"Ulterior motives?"

"What if the tiger is hungry one day? What if he asks the trees of the forest where he can make easy prey today, for example, by surprising a disgruntled chameleon and a naive sloth drinking on the shore of a lake?"

As if struck by lightning, the sloth wheeled around. Hastily, he searched the surroundings. He almost thought he felt the tiger's hot breath on the back of his neck and began to tremble involuntarily.

"Do you really think he would do such a shameful thing?" he croaked in panic.

"I don't know ... And that makes me nervous."

As always, the community of animals was well attended. The snake looked joyfully into the illustrious round. A tense expectation was in the air.

There was a waiting silence. All heads turned towards the tiger, the newest and most prominent member of their exchange.

"Why are you looking at me like that?" the big cat asked in wonder.

"Um ... I thought ... you ...", the snake stammered uncertainly.

Then the tiger laughed uproariously. "But aren't you the moderator of this community? I am lucky that you welcome me into your circle at all."

"Very well," hissed the snake with renewed confidence. "Then let us begin! Are there any suggestions for the agenda?"

The sloth and the chameleon almost rolled over to make their point first: "The dark side!" they shouted, completely out of breath. "The dark side of power!"

The snake gave the tiger and the elephant a sceptical look. "The dark side? What's that?"

The sloth nudged the chameleon frantically. "Come on, tell them!"

"No, you do it!" whispered the scaly reptile. "I don't dare!"

"Come on, you can explain it better!"

"But the tiger is there too ... I'm sure he'll take offence!"

Impatiently, the snake cleared his throat. "Now, do you want to explain what this is all about, or shall we adjourn this point?"

"Adjourn?" the chameleon repeated in a voice that was all squeaky with excitement. "No, absolutely not!"

On shaky feet, the reptile crawled into the middle of the circle and looked around, trembling.

"I think our new ways are really great," he began quietly. The chameleon was not at all used to being in the limelight. "But sometimes they also give me cause for concern. The forest now houses so much information. What if it all gets out of control?"

"But that is why we have developed a set of rules, so that we can control the diversity of information," interjected the elephant in his role as supreme governor.

"That's not what I mean," the chameleon explained. "I'm not about controlling how we ensure high quality information. I'm about controlling what we use the information for!"

The monkey scratched his head in confusion. "I don't understand!"

"We all have different interests. The predators want to eat. But I don't want to be eaten. I want to quench my thirst from safe waters. But this way I am predictable. The forest knows my habits. And now that we have these breakthrough predictive models, it's not hard to ask the trees when I'll be where to drink from a lake."

The animals of the forest hung on the chameleon's lips with sorrowful eyes. The reptile's gaze caught the tiger, proud and powerful. And deadly. "And that is ... I mean, if ..." The chameleon did not dare to speak out loudly.

The tiger took a step forward, strutting into the middle of the circle. "And that means that if a predator like me uses this information to predict your moves, we can ambush you and eat you."

"Exactly," sobbed the chameleon, and all the animals suffered with him.

"We understand you," the elephant said thoughtfully, turning to the chameleon. Then he raised his head, looking piercingly at each of them. The elephant's deep voice rumbled through the ranks. "But we must not bury our heads in the sand, we have to find a solution to the problem."

"That's how I see it too," the snake hissed. "Let's brainstorm together what a solution might look like."

And so it happened. The animals shouted their suggestions wildly. Until the thunderous roar of the tiger silenced them. "You can't understand your own words here! One after the other!"

"We need a code of honour!" cried the elephant.

"Exactly. And anyone who violates this code of honour will have the information withheld from them in future!" the sloth added.

"That sounds very good," agreed the tiger. "How about the elephant, in his role as governor, driving this proposal?"

The elephant nodded.

"And we need some kind of classification of the information," the rhino suggested next.

"What do you mean by classification?" the monkey wanted to know.

"We need to be clear about what information can only be used judiciously and falls under the code of honour."

"Good idea," decided the tiger. "Rhinoceros, do you want to deal with it directly?"

"Yes, I'd love to."

The snake told the chameleon to name his suggestions.

"You know I'm not the fastest, and I'm not a fighter either."

"But you have the best camouflage in the whole jungle!" praised the sloth.

"That's the way it is. And I wonder if it can't be done for the information as well."

"Camouflage?"

"Why not? In cases where it is only a question of how many animals use a drinking source, for example, you could disguise the identity of the animals. Thereby the core message doesn't lose value, but the possibilities of misusing the information are limited."

"I think that's an excellent idea," the tiger thought. "Please work out a detailed proposal of what that might look like."

"I'd love to," sniffled the chameleon. But this time he did not cry out of fear, but out of gratitude and relief.

Practical application:
In this chapter, the animals of the forest have addressed a whole range of important issues that inevitably go hand in hand with the development of a data culture.

The more you work with data, collect and use information, the more you have to deal with data protection and ethics.

So often in the history of mankind, the powerful have allowed themselves to be seduced by their power. And the data-driven company commands a power that opens up so many possibilities that it can also bring out dark sides.

Therefore, it is absolutely advisable to provide a clear moral compass as part of data governance that provides clear ethical guidance to employees and data users.

Also remember to involve the works council of your company. Because there is a very thin line between saving effort or costs by optimising work processes and the sensitive issue of employee monitoring. Give your works council a seat on the ethics committee to actively involve the employee representatives in the design.

But ethics is not the only issue. At the latest since the introduction of the General Data Protection Regulation in 2018, the legal framework of data protection must be addressed in addition to ethical issues. Involve your data protection officer closely in your data governance to ensure an appropriate legal framework for your data.

Here, in addition to guidelines, the masking of data, which the chameleon had suggested at the end of the chapter, can offer helpful approaches.

Lean and Fast

Curious, the cheetah roamed along the edge of the jungle. He had heard a sound that caught his attention. Like claws running over a tree bark again and again. Almost as if ... No, it couldn't be. The sounds were too regular, too long. No one was that persistent.

With a furrowed brow, the cheetah pushed the thicket a little to one side and peered through the opening of the refreshingly fragrant green branches.

His eyes widened in surprise. *This can't be true!* But there was indeed the bear standing there. Disgruntled, he scratched his head and shortly afterwards drew the next symbols in the bark of a tree with the sharp claws of his imposing paws.

Impressed, the cheetah looked around. Everywhere he saw tree trunks that bore witness to the bear's unswerving attempts. All of them were carved with stick figures, vague outlines of humans, images of plucked plants and dead animals.

What the heck is he up to? Has the bear gone mad?

Growling, the bear looked up into the treetops and his face contorted into a fierce grimace. The cheetah flinched in fright. A rumble of thunder echoed through the jungle. And once again, the bear's mighty fist smashed furiously into the shaking tree. "Nothing! Nothing! And nothing again!" he hissed, beside himself.

"Bear, my old friend," the cheetah said cautiously. The bear flinched and wheeled around with a piercing look in his eyes. "What are you so furious about? Normally, you bears are rather comfortable fellows ..."

Exhausted, the bear let his massive body plop to the ground and sighed deeply. "I've been trying to find a solution for days. Oh, what do I say, for weeks. But I just don't succeed!"

The cheetah eyed the bear anxiously. His eyes looked small, puffy, with deep circles around them. And he didn't look quite as heavy and massive as usual. "Tell me, have you lost weight?"

"I'm sure," growled the bear. "I haven't eaten for days. That's almost as bad as hibernation. But I haven't slept either."
"What's wrong with you?"
"I'm so worried!"
"What troubles you, my friend?"
"Soon it will be time for hibernation. What a bad timing!"
"Why? You do it every year."
"Yes, but we haven't found a way to stop the humans yet. If I go to sleep in a few weeks ... will I even wake up? Will our forest still be there?"
The cheetah compassionately placed a paw on the bear's broad shoulder. "I see. And what are you carving into the trees?"
"I'm looking for answers. For a solution."
"What exactly is your idea?"
"I am working on a complicated model of how we can drive the humans out of here once and for all."
"And how do you imagine that?"
"Quite simply ... What would drive us out of this jungle?"
The cheetah thought hard. *What would drive a bear from his home? Hunger, of course. What else?*
"Hunger?"
"Exactly! I'm working on predictive models of how we need to place animals in our jungle to take away their food source."
"So they'll retreat at some point?"
"Yes, exactly," the bear confirmed. "That's my idea. We starve them out. And drive them out of our forest."
The cheetah scratched his head thoughtfully. "I'm sorry to be the bearer of bad news. But I don't think it will work."
"No?" asked the bear. "But humans have to eat too!" He paused for a moment. "Don't they?"
"Yes, of course. But humans rarely eat wild animals like us."
"Then why are they hunting us?"
"I don't know. For the pleasure of killing, maybe."
The bear shook his head sadly. "Unbelievable, these humans."

"Yes, you're right," whispered the cheetah. "Their food is usually delivered to them. I've seen that before. There are these tin boxes on wheels and they bring the food and drink."

The bear scratched his head grumpily. With tears in his eyes, he surveyed the countless works of art he had so persistently scratched into the trees. "Then it was all for nothing? Then I could have eaten and drunk to my heart's content for days and slept uselessly for half the day, and been no further from a solution than after all this toil?"

"I think your basic idea is really great," the cheetah tried to rebuild his dejected friend.

"But how was I supposed to know ..."

The cheetah stared into the forest, brooding. "Yes, how could you have known. That's a great question, my dear bear. Because I think that's where we need to start."

"What do you mean?"

"We have to be flexible. And fast. Lean and fast!"

"Well, listen, just look at me! I'm a bear! Do I look lean and fast?" the bear growled with a sarcastic grin.

"You are welcome to stay as you are," laughed the cheetah. "But our actions must become leaner and faster."

The bear scratched his head. "I don't understand."

"Look, you had a great idea. But it's complicated, it has countless variables. And so you got a little lost, you spent days trying to find solutions. But maybe the solution goes in a slightly different direction. You've been walking stubbornly straight ahead. Probably you should have turned in a different direction on your elaborate journey."

"Hm, that may be. But I can only see that when I've tried it out."

"Yes, failure is part of the idea generation process. I agree with you there. But then we have to find ways not to fail after days of ordeals without food and sleep. We have to act lean and fast. And fail lean and fast!"

"That sounds good, even for a sluggish, fat, slow bear like me," growled the bear. "But how could I have failed any faster in my quest?"

The cheetah looked up at the sky, lost in thought. "How did you go about it?"

"Well, I had this idea of cutting off the food sources. And then I tried to develop a model that would tell me exactly how we could do that."

"But a model like that is incredibly complicated, isn't it?"

The bear let his eyes wander over the countless trees into which he had carved his many attempts and grinned broadly. "You can say that again!"

"How would it have been if you had first started to think about what information you needed for this?"

The bear nodded slowly. "Hm ... that sounds sensible."

"Then in the next step you could have checked whether this information was available at all."

"Oh yeah, right!"

"And if not, you could have adapted the idea right away without wasting much time."

"My goodness, what I could have chomped in that time!"

"And if the information is available, then a first aspect could have been picked out to test to what extent everything fits together."

The bear was ecstatic: "And with each of these small steps, I can easily adjust if something doesn't go the way I hoped it would."

"That's how even a bear becomes lean and fast," laughed the cheetah.

The bear slapped his forehead with his massive paw: "We must find the snake immediately! The community must know about this new approach!"

There was a rustling in the trees. And the snake dangled from a branch above the two stunned heads, grinning audaciously at the bear and cheetah. "No need," he purred, "I overheard everything. Tomorrow already, I will immediately convene the community of animals."

"Excellent," cried the cheetah. His bright eyes flashed challengingly at the bear. "Come with me, we must prepare for this."

And the bear trotted excitedly after the cheetah.

"Lean and fast," the snake hissed. "That could have been my idea!"

Practical application:

There are certainly many great ideas in your company too. And that's a good thing! The first step is to put ideas on the table. Promote a culture in which your colleagues talk openly about their ideas and create a framework in which ideas can be submitted and tested.

Unfortunately, in practice it is hardly possible to implement all ideas. The art is to select the right ideas.

This should first be done using a business case calculation. Focus on the ideas that promise the greatest benefit for your company.

Then you can push the most promising ideas with the cheetah's agile mindset. Be flexible, be fast, and be lean.

Innovative ideas and groundbreaking data projects carry the risk of failure. Even the most promising data science projects have so many variables that their outcome is not certain at the beginning. It is possible that the expected data patterns will not be found in the data after all.

Failure is part of the journey. And if the failure of a creative idea is viewed negatively in your corporate culture, then you are blocking innovation and creativity with this cultural attitude. A failed idea is only bitter if you have invested vast amounts of time, effort, energy and resources in an endeavour without realising that you are getting further and further lost and not even beginning to achieve the lofty goals.

The trick is to fail fast. And you can do that by starting your data projects small and lean. Calculate the business case. It's simple, quick and no big effort.

The business case is good? Then don't immediately set up a mammoth project with an uncertain outcome. Proceed step by step and start with the least possible complexity. Is the required data even available? Do the data sets have the required quality? Check in manageable pilots whether the expected data patterns are really reflected in the data. Then you can launch a first small data product (MVP - "Minimal Viable Product").

All these steps have confirmed how great the idea is and prove its practical feasibility? Then you can develop your Minimal Viable Product step by step, create operational structures, automate the data loads and operationalise the data product.

By the way, if the small steps signal to you that you have taken the wrong path, this does not necessarily mean that you have to discard your idea completely. On your agile journey you can develop ideas further, readjust and adapt them. And who knows, maybe your final project will be even bigger, better and more profitable than the first spark that set the process in motion.

The Power of Manipulation

"We thank the bear and the cheetah for their explanations," the snake hissed. "This new method will save us a lot of effort in the future. And it will help us focus on what is important. What a great contribution! And with that, I end our exchange today and wish you a safe journey back to your territory."

The animals left the meeting place at the dolphin's lagoon. But the tiger remained sitting pensively in his spot, staring into the glowing sun setting on the horizon. The dolphin peered out from the surface of the water and eyed the majestic king of the jungle. Slowly, the bear, the cheetah and the parrot came closer.

"What's on your mind?" the wise dolphin opened the conversation in his bright, clear voice.

"I don't know," murmured the tiger, unable to take his eyes off the distant sunset. "It's a little spark that stirs inside me. A thought that I cannot grasp yet."

"Like we missed something?" the parrot asked.

"Yes. Maybe."

"I feel the same way," the cheetah confirmed, grabbing his heart with his sleek paw. "The solution is in here. But I feel like it's not finding its way into my head!"

"It's about time!" the parrot warned. "I've been watching the humans from the air. They continue to spread. Unstoppable. Mercilessly. And they leave devastation and death wherever they go!"

"How long do we have?" growled the bear. Concern spoke from his deep voice.

"We won't make it through the coming winter," the parrot replied, lowering his head dejectedly. "Too many trees will be cut down. Too many habitats destroyed."

"The bear's intention was good," the tiger interjected. His gaze was still fixed on the distance, as if he thought he saw a solution there. "Very good, in fact. Probably we can't fight the humans. But finding a way to drive them away, that's a smart thought."

"And a hopeless one at that," the bear stated dryly.

"There is always hope," the tiger announced in a calm, kind voice. "There is still some time."

"But we've already tried everything!"

Compassionately, the dolphin considered the bear. "Certainly we have come a long way, my friend. We have learned to gather many pieces of information and trust in them. And so we searched in vain for information that would help us stop the humans. When we did not find it, we developed prophetic models to predict their actions. But this endeavour was also in vain. What is the next step on our path? How can we evolve once again?"

All eyes were fixed on the dolphin. Even the tiger took his eyes off the sunset. With furrowed brow, he stared at the dolphin's kind face. And in the faithful eyes he read the answer. "The bear was already on the right track. We've been asking the wrong question all along!"

"What do you mean?" the cheetah breathed.

"We have focused too much on predicting what the humans will do."

"But what else could we have focused on?"

The tiger beamed all over his face. "We must not allow the humans to steer us through their next steps. Rather, we must try to influence the humans's behaviour so that they act in a way that suits our goals!"

The bear's sad face suddenly brightened. He rose. And slumped down again. "But my idea of cutting off their food supply is not working. It's hopeless! So hopeless!"

"Because all you ever think about is food!" the parrot teased. "Maybe their food is invulnerable. Then we'll just have to find other ways to drive them away."

"And what would that be?"

"The information of the forest will show us the way," the dolphin announced solemnly.

"But we have already searched them. And found nothing!"

"Then we have to broaden our horizons."

"The dolphin is talking in riddles again!" the bear rumbled.

"No, the dolphin is showing us the way!" The tiger laughed rancorously. "The information of our forest cannot answer this question. Because we will not find the solution to a problem that has never before existed in our jungle here." Nodding, he stroked the scar on his flank with his velvety paw. "And it is not the first time we have been confronted with such a situation."

The bear stared uncomprehendingly from the tiger to the dolphin and resignedly buried his face in his mighty paws. The cheetah frowned as he tried to comprehend the words. But there was a sparkle in the parrot's eyes and a knowing smile played around his yellow beak. "I'll summon the hummingbirds immediately!"
And the dolphin nodded contentedly at the parrot and the tiger.

With his head held high, the tiger stood in front of a buzzing flock of hummingbirds. The glowing red evening sun framed his black and yellow striped face. The fangs flashed as he opened his huge mouth and began to speak.
"Once again we need your help, my tireless friends! Once before you saved me. And today, the survival of our beloved jungle is at stake. Flap your wings, brave hummingbirds! Fly forth and once again find other forests in faraway lands."
Excitedly, the hummingbirds fluttered up and down, back and forth. Proudly they held the twigs from the Sunny Glade in their little beaks, with which they could pick up and carry information thanks to the unicorn's magic. "What shall we look for this time?"
"We are looking for forests from which humans have been successfully evicted. Any information from these forests can help us understand why humans have taken flight. Find them. And you will be the saviours of our jungle."
And the flock of hummingbirds took to the skies. Their tiny wings carried them south and north, east and west. And the thoughts of the animals of the jungle were with them.
"Fly fast, my little friends. For time is running short ..."

Practical application:
Information and data are knowledge. And knowledge is power.
The ability to analyse and interpret data from the past is therefore a powerful tool.

We have seen in the previous chapters that predicting the future based on data is even more effective than understanding the past.

In this chapter, however, the animals of the jungle go one more step further. Instead of foreseeing the future, they develop a plan to bring about, to enforce the future they desire. This results in concrete recommendations for action.

The use of data cannot be more powerful than this endeavour!

Not every use case is suitable for prescriptive analytics. Nevertheless, it is worthwhile to sharpen your focus on the cases in which there is an opportunity for use. You should not leave such opportunities unused in your company.

Where do you see the potential in your company to optimise behaviour and actions? Which kind of data can support you in this?

Summary Part 4

Although the animals of the forest had already achieved a data-driven jungle with a mature data culture, they still had to face new questions and challenges.

With the increasing use of data, it was necessary to deal more thoroughly with questions of data ethics and data protection in order to ensure professional handling of information.

Following the agile principle of "fail fast", the animals developed a new methodology to quickly, leanly and purposefully avoid getting bogged down in new ideas at great expense without first piloting their added value and feasibility.

With the expansion of their horizons in the direction of prescriptive analytics, the animals of the jungle are now taking a further step that powerfully rounds off the possibilities available to them.

Part 5

... in which the animals of the forest finally reap the fruits of their data-driven journey.

The Rescue of the Jungle

Fatigue reflected in their eyes. But the hummingbirds continued to flutter bravely, whirring their nimble wings over the treetops of the jungle. And in their little beaks they held solemnly the many branches in which they had stored information from all over the world that would decide the salvation and disaster of the jungle.

All the animals of the forest were gathered in the Sunny Glade. It was the birthplace of their community, where the unicorn had brought the information of the jungle to life with her dazzling magic.

The silence was eerie. There was neither wind nor cracking branches. The animals held their breath. And hundreds of pairs of eyes were transfixed on the swooping hummingbirds. One after the other, they sailed across the clearing and rammed their branch deep into the mossy earth of the forest.

The tiger strode proudly through the rows. The animals quickly stepped aside and reverently bowed their heads. Like a symbol of strength, the mighty big cat let his fiery eyes roam through the crowd. Then, with a smile, the tiger fixed on the countless hummingbirds that had settled exhaustedly on the grass in the heart of the Sunny Glade, gasping for breath.

"My brave little friends. Once again you have done a faithful service to our jungle that we will certainly not forget. Thank you! The information has been connected. Now let us hope they hold a solution to the many mysteries."

And the cheetah and the jaguar set to work. They narrowed their eyes, thoughtfully circled the mightiest tree at the edge of the clearing, extended their razor-sharp claws and carved the first signs into the ancient bark.

"Lean and fast, my old companion!" cried the cheetah.

"Shall we start by looking for patterns of results?"

"My thought exactly!"

Their eyes flashed as they studied the treetops. And finally the cheetah nodded to the tiger.

"We found something," he whispered into the tense silence.

"Tell us!"

"We have identified eleven forests that all have one thing in common. Once they too were threatened by humans, who destroyed habitats and spread inexorably. But miraculously, humans have left the areas in flight."

The tiger felt hot and cold at the same time. "What for?" he croaked. "What has brought about this miracle?"

"Step by step. Lean and fast," the cheetah shouted, turning back to the jaguar. "Let's keep going!"

And they researched the information, tirelessly scratching symbols into the thick bark.

"Haven't you found anything yet?" the tiger urged, stepping from one leg to the other.

"Yes ... No ... It's ..."

"Now tell me!"

"We have something ...", the jaguar stammered.

"But it doesn't make sense," the cheetah added, pale as a sheet.

"Speak up!" the tiger thundered, and the sight of his deadly fangs made the animals' blood run cold.

"Humans," whispered the cheetah. "It was the humans themselves."

"But what does that mean?" the bear growled, scratching his head in confusion.

"Humans came. And then they left the forest and stopped the project."

"In all eleven forests?"

"Yes, without exception."

"But why?"

"That's what we have to find out," the cheetah declared, stepping up to the tree again.

The tiger closed his eyes tensely. He could no longer watch the jaguar and the cheetah scratching sketch after sketch into the bark. Tireless and creative. Lean, fast and persistent.

Then the two cats stepped into the middle of the circle. The shadows of the setting sun settled over the clearing. They paused one last time. Enjoyed the tension of the moment.

"If you wait any longer, I'll eat both of you alive," growled the tiger.

The cheetah grinned broadly. "They are organisations. Humans who stand up for animals and draw attention to the boundless injustice. They stand up against the evil humans."

"Then why don't they kill their enemies like they tried to do with our tiger?"

"Because humans don't kill other humans."

"And these human protests cause the bad humans to leave our jungle?"

"If the organisation is big enough, we can hope for that."

Thoughtfully, the tiger looked around. "But how do we make these organisations aware of our predicament?"

"That's a question we couldn't get from the information," the cheetah confessed.

Thoughtful silence fell over the clearing as the animals of the forest pondered intently.

"We would need someone who can speak the language of humans. Unfortunately, they don't understand us animals," the elephant muttered.

Then all eyes turned to the parrot sitting innocently on the stump of a fallen tree, hopping restlessly up and down.

"And so we have come full circle," the tiger announced in a gentle voice. "With the parrot's words our long journey began, and with his words it will end. You have brought the community together, spreading the gospel of information throughout the jungle. Now take our message out into the world and get help, my faithful friend!"

And the parrot spread his colourful wings. A gentle breeze followed him, like the breath of fate. With open mouths, the animals gazed after him. And the parrot flew faster and further than ever before in his life.

Seven days later, the animals of the jungle celebrated a lavish feast. The parrot had once again done a great job as the mouthpiece of the jungle. The elephant had pounded a huge mountain of fermented apples into slush especially for this celebration. And the animals had mixed the powerful juice with the purest drinking water in the forest.

The cosy, sweet scent filled the Sunny Glade. The orange-red light of the evening sun fading on the horizon danced with the shadows of the towering treetops. And this time there was no tense silence. The animals were talking wildly, celebrating in each other's arms and toasting each other with proudly swelling chests.

"To our tiger!"

"And to the parrot!"

"Stop, to the governor!"

"What about the cheetah?"

"And to the dolphin, who unfortunately has to celebrate alone in his lagoon!"

"Here's to all of us!" the tiger thundered with a joyful roar.

Then he sat down lonely at the edge of the clearing and silently enjoyed watching the exuberant hustle and bustle of the cheerful crowd. *We have achieved a lot*, he thought contentedly. *And if I hadn't been such a stubborn fool, we would have done it even sooner.*

He thought of his long discussions with the hippo. Even now, the stubborn hippo had not brought himself to bite the bullet and acknowledge the power of information. *Sad that one can close one's eyes to the world so much. But one will probably never be able to convince every single one.*

The tiger heard the soft rustling of grass. And when he looked up, he saw the parrot, the elephant and the cheetah coming towards him.

"What's the matter, your majesty? Don't you feel like celebrating?" asked the parrot.

"Yes, yes," the tiger replied, sipping his drink with a dreamy look. "I just wanted to recall the past few days."

The elephant amicably put his trunk around the parrot's shoulders. "The fact that our little chatterbox was able to animate two animal welfare organisations at once was quite an achievement!"

"Did you see how quickly the humans fled when they put their protest signs in their way?" the cheetah recalled, beaming.

"And they were scared to death of those strange tin boxes!" laughed the tiger.

"They are called cameras," the parrot explained. "Humans are as magical as the unicorn. Supposedly, they can use these cameras to send images all over the world. And spread the displeasure of the misdeeds in our jungle even further."

"No wonder the villains fled so quickly when faced with such sorcery."

They all sipped their drink and the parrot fainted into the grass.

"Is this the end of our project?" the elephant asked melancholically.

"No," whispered the tiger. "This is just the beginning! It goes on and on."

Practical application:
In this chapter, the animals of the jungle ultimately deployed all their skill. They again tapped external sources of information, made data pattern-based evaluations and, in the end, set up a

successful prescriptive analytics use case with which they could actively set events in motion that secured their habitat.

New and exciting in this chapter, however, is the end. Because in successful data projects, one final step is often forgotten.

Celebrate your success!

Communicate the success stories!

And use them as a basis for the next lighthouse projects by inspiring other teams and colleagues with practical and tangible success stories.

Because in the wise words of the converted tiger, "It goes on and on!"

A New Morning

"After that, I don't know what happened," grumbled the tiger, amused. "Probably the fermented apple juice was a little too strong after all."

"That sounds like a memorable celebration," smiled the dolphin, who had clearly enjoyed the tale of the victory celebrations.

"Yes, it was."

Silently, the tiger stared out at the water. The waves rippled gently in the light breeze. And the sun conjured up a sparkling play of lights on the rippling water surface.

The dolphin eyed the satisfied predatory cat. "Where do we go from here?"

His voice was clear and bright. From them spoke a pure wisdom that the tiger had always underestimated in the long months of his stubborn, blind behaviour. "I don't know," he said slowly. "At first it was a feeling of euphoria when we achieved our targets. But now there's a strange emptiness. An impatience that makes my heartbeat race."

"You want to go on ... achieve even more ..."

The tiger nodded, lost in thought. "Yes, I probably do."

The two animals gazed dreamily into the horizon, enjoying the picturesque silence of the lagoon and indulging in their own thoughts.

"How can we go on now? We fought off the threat from humans at the last moment, the animals never had more to eat and better quality drinking water. The whole jungle is growing and thriving. I think we are clearly better off than any other forest on earth."

Then the dolphin's clever eyes flashed and excited clicking sounds came out of his snout. "Tiger, you are a genius!"

"But I still have no idea how we can continue."

"Yes, you do," the dolphin grinned mischievously. "You just don't know it yet."

"So sometimes you really scare me."

"Hearing that from a mighty tiger fills me with pride," laughed the dolphin. "But seriously, you had the brilliant idea! We are clearly better off than any other forest on earth! Don't you understand what that means?"

The tiger rolled his eyes in confusion. "It's probably because of the treacherous fermented apple juice that I can't think clearly yet. But no, I don't understand that!" he growled sullenly.

"Then hold on! If we animals here in the jungle are better off than animals in other forests, then we have something to be envied by everyone. Don't we?"

"Yeah, sure."

"And we managed to do all that through the information in our forest. Correct?"

"Of course."

"Surely then the other forests would be highly interested in learning from us and benefiting from our pioneering achievements."

The tiger's eyes widened. "And for that, they would certainly be willing to reciprocate. More food! Foreign plants! Anything our hearts desire!"

The dolphin nodded contentedly and exuberantly splashed a load of water into the tiger's beaming face.

"I could offer my data academy in other lands. The lagoon is easily accessible for fish and birds. And as a sea creature, I am very mobile and can easily visit foreign waters and pass on our knowledge, laying the foundation for the use of information."

"And with experienced experts like the cheetah and jaguar, we could do analysis for other forests and have the results brought to them by the hummingbirds using branches."

"The elephant is definitely good at communicating his models for roles and responsibilities."

"And the parrot becomes our mouthpiece, selling our achievements in the other forests and arousing their interest!"

The tiger proudly raised his head and sniffed the refreshing salty breeze of the sea bordering the lagoon. It smelled of freedom. Of success. Of future!

"I'm about to call a meeting," he announced solemnly, his eyes twinkling as if he were on the prowl. "We must get started immediately and make further plans. For there is much to do!"

Practical application:
Many use cases that involve the sale of data or analytics to external stakeholders start as internal use cases. From the point of view of the required maturity, which an external data product should definitely have, this is a reasonable procedure.

So feel free to check for your best data products: What is the added value of the data product? Is this added value only interesting for your company? Which partners or competitors, customers or suppliers could also benefit from this information, so that they might even be willing to pay money for your information?

Whether one actually wants to offer data products to the outside world or considers data and analytics to be primarily an internal topic is a question each company must answer for itself.

However, when asking this question, bear in mind that the external reuse of internal data products in particular is a very efficient and elegant way to maximise and multiply (through additional target groups) the monetary added value of a good idea.

What role do you want data products to play in your business?

Summary Part 5

At the end of the story, the animals of the forest deploy all their skill they have developed in their data-driven jungle.

With their newly acquired knowledge, skills and methods, they use the forest's information to protect their habitat from the threat of humans.

At the end, they have a well-deserved party and ponder how they can get even more out of their achievements - for example, by selling data and services to other forests.

The use of prescriptive analytics is not necessary for every business problem. Every idea and every use case requires a different component from the data-driven method box.

The possibilities of how data can enable added value for you are almost unlimited.

It's your data-driven journey. What do you want to achieve with your data?

20 Steps to Success

With the fable "Data for the Tiger", you have now completed a long and hopefully also instructive, exciting and entertaining journey through the wide-ranging world of data culture.

Based on this beastly story, you were allowed to experience all the development steps from the founding of the data-driven jungle company to the implementation of highly complex prescriptive analytics use cases based on external data sources at first hand.

For few established companies, the journey to becoming a data-driven company starts at the very beginning. Surely you have a solid status quo on which to build and develop your data culture.

The following step-by-step guide summarises the most important insights from this fable once again in twenty steps. Think of this list as a kind of checklist in which you determine your starting point and which you can use as an inspiring impulse for your next steps.

1: Send a clear message in your company: "Those who are poorly informed die out".

2: Develop a data strategy with a clear objective and concrete, tangible sub-goals.

3: Aim for the highest possible level of automation.

4: Use visualisation standards to ensure that data and reports are comparable and interpretable.

5: Increase the data literacy of your colleagues in a targeted way.

6: Develop a value-added data governance model and roll it out across the organisation.

7: Understand communication as an important culture driver.

8: Empower power users through self-service analytics.

9: Use communities as data culture drivers.

10: Establish a data catalogue as a foundation for the democratisation of data.

11: Convince the doubters in your company through tangible lighthouse projects with measurable added value.

12: Convince your company's leaders of the value of your data-driven journey.

13: Check whether external data sources can profitably complement your internal data stocks.

14: Build a data science team and add value to your data with predictive analytics.

15: Drive a data-driven and fact-based leadership and decision-making culture.

16: Do not underestimate issues such as data protection and ethics.

17: Act lean and fast. Fail lean and fast. Work with MVPs and pilots.

18: Watch out for powerful prescriptive analytics use cases.

19: Celebrate and communicate your success stories.

20: Maximise your added value by selling data and analytics as external data products.

The BARC Data Culture Framework
(by Dr. Carsten Bange)

The data-driven company is a declared goal of many enterprises. But it is a rocky road. It is often not clear what really belongs to a data strategy and that the lack of a data culture can condemn any approach to a data strategy to failure.

According to the BARC study „BARC Data Culture Survey 22" [1], 97 % of all companies consider data strategy and data culture to be relevant. However, in practice, although companies want to derive more business value from data, the need for investment and change as well as the resulting benefits are often too intangible.

One reason for this are the numerous obstacles on the way to establishing a sustainable data culture: data is isolated in silos, systems for decision support are too ineffective. There is a lack of data and skills for data-based decisions, processes and products. The implementation of data quality, data security and data protection is challenging.

In addition to defining a data and analytics strategy and making the necessary technology investments, organisations must also undergo a cultural transformation to a data-driven corporate culture - the data culture. Otherwise, both strategy and technology lack the necessary environment to unfold their potential.

What is a data culture?

Data culture is a sub-area or characteristic of corporate culture. Here, culture refers to all shared values, social norms and ways of thinking that determine the behaviour of the organisation's members among each other and in their effect on the outside world.

A data-driven corporate culture treats data as an important resource that significantly influences actions and decisions at all

---

[1] see BARC Data Culture Survey 2022

levels of the organisation, all the way to the company's business model.

While companies have always been interested in their metrics and individual data usage, with a data culture, data is used on a broader level and influences how members of the organisation communicate and collaborate with each other.

Goals and effects of a data culture

Data culture cannot be bought or prescribed. It emerges through various influencing factors such as organisational structure, rewarded or sanctioned behaviour or communication and decision-making by managers. The emergence of a data culture can be actively supported, especially by addressing the approaches systematised in the BARC Data Culture Framework (see below).

The main goal is to empower all employees to actively use data. This not only facilitates their daily work, but also fully exploits the company's potential. Because through the active use of data, decisions become more successful, initiatives more effective and competitive advantages clearer.

Essential starting points for establishing a data culture are three levels: the strategic level of the business model, the dispositive level of decision-making and the operational level of ongoing process execution and improvement.

Why a data-driven corporate culture is important

Before meaningful change can be made, it is important to know the benefits and outcomes that can be achieved. Initiatives towards a data-driven culture are no exception. Respondents to the BARC Data Culture Survey 22 were most likely to have used data to improve decision-making, reduce costs and improve processes. Other benefits achieved by a data culture include increased revenue, better acceptance of decisions, a shared understanding of data and also improved competitiveness.

Towards a successful data culture with the BARC Data Culture Framework: A framework with concrete starting points for companies

The BARC Data Culture Framework was developed to help organisations understand the key starting points for establishing and improving a data culture. The framework contains six areas of action that can be addressed.

There is no inherent hierarchy among the different aspects; different starting points are important for each company. However, data access and data governance are among the first issues that most companies address. But communication about and with data is also a good first starting point, as it can influence the behaviour of people and thus the culture of the company.

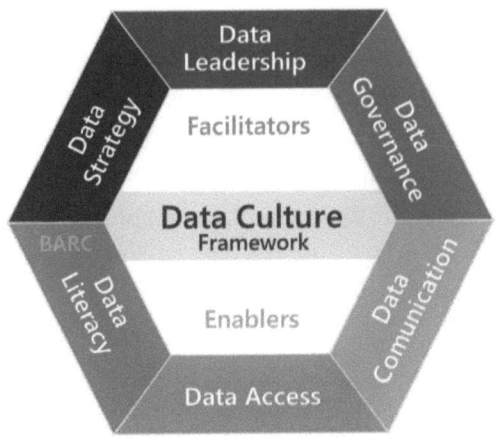

Facilitators: Must-haves for data-driven companies

The upper half of the framework, the so-called „facilitators", describes must-haves for every company that wants to be data-driven.

Data Leadership

Data leadership describes the behaviour of managers with regard to data and analytics. Definition of targets, organisational structure and process design as well as creating accountability for data are essential aspects here. Authentic leadership always starts with the actions and commitment shown by the leaders themselves. Therefore, they themselves should set a shining example of how to be data-driven, for example fact-based decisions and communication. Not to be underestimated is also the task of the leaders to provide the necessary resources for data and analytics (especially personnel, time and money) and to enforce essential aspects in case of conflict, for example the opening of data silos.

Data Strategy

The strong consideration of the data culture in the data strategy is also essential for the establishment of a data culture. A holistic data strategy takes into account business, organisational and technical aspects for a description of the desired target state and the way to get there. A successful data strategy pays off on the strategic goals of the company. The establishment of a data culture is elementary for this, because the company's data culture defines the boundaries of the data strategy. A data strategy cannot drive anything forward if the data culture is not developed accordingly. In this respect, influencing the data culture should be an inherent and important part of the data strategy.

Data Governance

Data governance encompasses people as well as processes and technologies required to manage and protect corporate data assets. The goal of data governance is to ensure universally understandable, accurate, complete, trustworthy, secure and discoverable corporate data. This data quality forms the basis of all further activities and ensures that operational processes run seamlessly and can best serve decision-making. The focus in building data governance should be on defining policies that set the necessary boundaries for activities with data, but at the same time support a positive atmosphere for the use of data and analytics as well as new use cases. Most importantly, responsibilities around data need to be defined with a particular focus on improving data quality and breaking down data silos. These are the two biggest obstacles to a positive data culture and even digitisation as a whole.

Enablers pave the way for data culture among employees

The lower half of the BARC Data Culture Framework deals with the so-called „enablers". Elements of this category aim to involve as many people as possible in organisations, the essential bearers of a corporate culture. It is only through them that the data culture is filled with life.

Data Access

The first sub-item is data access. Data must be made accessible and comprehensible. Organisational regulations with regard to data access must also be observed and the necessary competences for access and use must be available (see below: Data Literacy).

The data discovery process in particular is of crucial importance. This is because a new understanding of roles is needed. From now on, it is the responsibility of the data producer to provide easily understandable descriptions (metadata) for everyone in the company, for example in data catalogues.

Data access is a cornerstone in data-driven companies. This is because it must be possible to use data from complex and distributed data landscapes in order to generate value from it. The biggest challenge lies in empowering business users to make sense of this data. Often they don't even know what data exists in their organisation. Or they don't understand the data or its context. In addition to creating technical access to the data, both the transparency of the data, for example in data catalogues, and the knowledge of the data are therefore of great importance for any good data culture.

Data Communication

It usually takes many stakeholders to communicate as broadly and comprehensively as possible about data. In doing so, leaders should explain how data and analytics drive business strategy and be clear about the importance of sharing data, applying analytics and AI, and developing data products or even data-driven business models. The CDO and / or all data and analytics leaders should have the skills to market data products and success stories in a way that makes clear where data and analytics help the business. Most importantly, sharing among colleagues should be encouraged through community building as well as the public presentation of successful data projects - because stories influence the culture immensely.

Data Literacy

By data literacy we mean the ability to find, evaluate, prepare, analyse and visualise data with appropriate tools, as well as to communicate using data and interpret analysis results. This is because in order to develop a long-term and broad educational approach to competence development in many different areas, it is important to ensure that competence development is not only directed at employees who already work with data, but also involves almost everyone in the organisation. It is important that the focus is not only on how to obtain and understand data, but also on how to analyse, use and communicate it. BARC also contributes to data literacy: If you want to learn even more about the topic of data culture, listen to our „Data Culture Podcast". In this podcast, Carsten Bange, CEO of BARC, presents together with guests from different industries how people and organisations create an effective data culture with data, analytics and AI.

How to start?

The BARC Data Culture Framework is the central content of the process model for establishing and improving the data culture in your organisation. We recommend - and are happy to support you in this - starting with an analysis of the six fields of action to determine to what extent they already promote or perhaps also hinder the data culture of the company. On this basis, fields of action can be prioritised and professional, technical and organisational measures can be derived. One thing should always be taken into account: A data culture does not change sustainably overnight or through a project. Establishing a positive data culture is a long-term task that requires goals and perseverance. But it is worth it. Because „culture is not everything, but everything is nothing without culture".

Further information: barc.com

Acknowledgements

My first thanks go to you, the readers of this data-driven fable. I hope this book has given you one or the other helpful impulse and also entertained you well. If you liked „Data for the Tiger", I would be very happy if you rate the book at a web shop and recommend the book to your colleagues.

Of course, I would also like to take this opportunity to thank all those who have actively supported me in writing this data culture fable.

Firstly, my thanks go to Tanja Müller, who once again created a great cover for the book.

Then I would like to express my sincere thanks to the two test readers Dr. Katarzyna Lasinska and Petra Embacher, whose constructive helpful feedback has significantly increased the quality of this book.

I would also like to thank Herbert Stauffer and Dr. Carsten Bange from BARC very much for their feedback, support and good cooperation.

Especially for the English version of this fable, I would like to thank the team of Deepl. I have used this translation service as a foundation, which I then reviewed and adapted myself before asking my colleagues Tim Ellis and Milica Radojicic for a final native speaker and translator review in order to ensure the highest possible translation quality. Many thanks, Milica and Tim, for your great and thorough feedback.

Finally, special thanks to my colleagues in my employer's data and analytics team, who have been with me on our data-driven journey for 13 years now. It is a great pleasure to work with you!